WEIRD & WACKY, Strange & Slimy

Written by Bonnie Bruno

Illustrated by Kevin Brown

Standard®
PUBLISHING

Cincinnati, Ohio

Dedication

For my family, whose love and encouragement keep me mindful of what matters most in life.

Published by Standard Publishing, Cincinnati, Ohio. www.standardpub.com.

Project editors: Robert Irvin, Dawn Korth
Cover design: Tobias' Outerwear for Books, Brigid Naglich
Interior design: Tobias' Outerwear for Books, Edie Freudenberger

Scripture taken from the *HOLY BIBLE, NEW INTERNATIONAL READER'S VERSION®*. *NIrV.*® Copyright © 1994, 1996 by Biblica, Inc.™ Used by permission of Zondervan. All rights reserved.

ISBN 978-0-7847-1865-0

15 14 13 12 11 10   2 3 4 5 6 7 8 9 10

Library of Congress Cataloging-in-Publication Data

Bruno, Bonnie.
  Weird & wacky, strange & slimy / written by Bonnie Bruno ; illustrated by Kevin Brown.
     p. cm.
  ISBN 978-0-7847-1865-0 (perfect bound)
  1. Nature--Religious aspects--Christianity--Juvenile literature. I. Brown, Kevin. II. Title. III. Title: Weird and wacky, strange and slimy.
   BT695.5.B78 2009
   231.7'65--dc22

                                              2009002330

Psssst! Wanna Know a Secret?

If you have access to the Internet, here's a Web site especially for you! You can visit the *Weird & Wacky, Strange & Slimy* Web site for interactive fun. Learn more about God's amazing world!

To access the site, type the following URL in your browser window:
http://www.bonniebruno.com/wwss.html

When Trouble Hits, I Click 'n' Flip

God created me with a hard shell and six legs. He gave me joints similar to the joints you have in your knees and elbows. I need joints to bend my six legs so I can safely crawl along branches. I also need claws at the end of each leg. Without claws, I would not be able to cling to branches and leaves or crawl through wet and slippery grass.

God knew there would be times I would slip and fall. He knew that I would need a way to pick myself up again. So he gave me a special spine on the bottom of my middle section. The spine fits into a little groove on my underbelly. If I accidentally fall and land upside down, I just arch my body like an athlete and flip right side up again with a quick *CLICK!* How clever is *that?*

And if a hungry critter wanders into my territory, my set of antennae picks up his sound and movement. I tuck my antennae and legs close to my body and lie very still. My enemy thinks I'm dead and loses interest fast! I can do this for hours if I need to until danger passes.

God thought of everything when he created me—**Click Beetle.**

Tell a Friend

Everybody has problems now and then. Problems don't have to flip us around, though! God is our helper, and he promises to be there for us always.

Read About It

"I trust in God. I praise his word. I trust in God. I will not be afraid. What can people do to me?"—Psalm 56:4

Pray About It

Thanks, God, for watching over me night and day.

One of my cousins has two false eyes— big round spots on its head that scare away predators.

Wrinkled for a Reason

My friends call me Slimy Sal. I'm a 30-inch chocolate-colored critter that looks like something out of a science fiction movie. Most members of my species are just four to six inches long, but at five feet, I'm king of the river. In fact, my appearance is so bizarre, fishermen have tossed their reels into the water when they've accidentally hooked me.

My favorite nesting area is in muddy crevices along the riverbanks here in China. I never just plop down for a nap, though. Instead, God taught me to always lie in my crevice facing outward in order to both feed and defend myself. Nothing can pass by without my knowing it. My body gets its needed oxygen from the bubbling waters of fast-moving streams and rivers. The sides of my head and body are covered in deep wrinkles that capture oxygen-rich water in pools so my body can absorb it.

I am a nocturnal hunter, meaning I hunt only after nightfall. I lie stone-still in about a foot of water, waiting for a turtle or fish to wander by. Then I explode through the water with my mouth wide open, ready to snatch unsuspecting prey in one big gulp. I also have an appetite for shrimp, snakes, crabs, and frogs. If need be, I am able to open one side of my mouth at a time (can you do that?). If my prey is large, I adjust my jaw by bending it forward like a gigantic scoop.

God thought of everything when he created me—**Chinese Giant Salamander.**

Tell a Friend

No matter our size, we can become a "giant" in God's eyes. How? By reading and obeying his Word and sharing his love with those around us.

Read About It

"Lord, you are everything I need. I have promised to obey your words."—Psalm 119:57

Pray About It

Lord, I want to obey your Word. Give me the courage to stand up tall for you.

Here in China, I am considered a delicacy at local fish markets.

What's for Dinner?

I'm a hungry plant that grows only in wet areas like waterlogged meadows or bogs. If you visit me in the springtime, I'll wow you with my purple petals and yellow *sepals* (these are small leaves that cup the bottom of a flower). The rest of the year, though, I'm just a bundle of tightly packed leaves. I look like a giant green apostrophe attached to a thick, greenish-yellow stalk. My speckly purple or reddish top stands out from the surrounding plants, and I usually grow to a height of 10 to 20 inches.

My stalk looks harmless enough, but if you are an insect, watch out! Under my colorful, curved hood lies a hidden passageway—a secret opening into my stalk. Like a dainty dessert, my stalk is lined with sweet nectar, luring buggy types inside for a taste. Once I capture them, I invite them to wander deeper into my hollow tube, where they can try to escape. I trick the insects with fake areas that appear to be exits. But these areas really lead deeper into my deadly stalk. Thick clumps of downward-pointing hairs prevent the insects from returning to the top of the stalk.

At the bottom lies a pool of water—and no escape. The water is fitted with bacteria that liquefy the insects, turning them into nitrogen. That makes them easy to digest. *Yum!* Dinner has never tasted so good!

God thought of everything when he created me—**Cobra Lily.**

Tell a Friend

The Cobra Lily tricks visitors to step inside, then entraps them. Temptation is like that too, but God is always there to help when we call on him.

Read About It

"He himself suffered when he was tempted. Now he is able to help others who are being tempted."—Hebrews 2:18

My real name is Darlingtonia californica, but people call me Cobra Lily because my hood reminds them of a cobra snake. I live mostly on the west coast of the United States, in California and Oregon.

Pray About It

Lord, thank you for being there to help me turn my back on temptation.

Call Me Talkative, But Please Don't Call Me "Polly!"

Elegant ladies of the 1800s used to dress up in their finest clothes, then take formal portraits with parrots like me. In those days, ships would bring parrots from our homeland in Africa to Europe. They'd stuff us into small compartments that were much too cramped. Life was unfair.

Today, I have been called a perfect mixture of brains and beauty, but don't ask me to chirp, "Polly want a cracker?" *Harrumph!* Yes, I am a parrot, but my history goes back much farther than Polly. I am like a voice recorder and can repeat multiple lines of songs or prayers. God gave me the rare ability to imitate speech and sounds. If a phone rings, I can copy the ring. The same is true if I hear a chainsaw or microwave running. And watch out—I will repeat messages on an answering machine again and again.

Although my cousins are spread across the world, I live in the lowland forests of central Africa. I move to the open country to feed with my flock. We fly high above the treetops screeching. You would never guess we are shy birds.

We lunch on nuts, fruits, berries, and seeds. We climb from one branch to another, and save most of our flying for the return trip to our roosting tree. Members of my species live to seventy years of age or older.

God thought of everything when he created me—**African Grey Parrot.**

Tell a Friend

This parrot is entertaining, but doesn't know that sometimes it's better to be quiet. The same is true for us when we pray. Try talking less and instead spending more time in silence. Think about God's love and forgiveness and give thanks for all he's done for you.

Read About It

"Be still, and know that I am God. I will be honored among the nations. I will be honored in the earth."—Psalm 46:10

One of my relatives was captured in 1958 near Uganda, and by 1977 he had a vocabulary of nearly one thousand words!

Pray About It

Lord, knowing you is an awesome thought! Please remind me to turn off the chatter and listen to you when I pray.

A Face Only a Mom Could Love

If you could request your favorite foods all in one meal, what would you eat? I would order fish, fish, and more fish!

I'm a member of the bat family with the official name of *Noctilio leporinus.* Members of my species live mostly in Central and South America. I'm known for my unusual face, which is shaped like a bulldog.

Who needs a fishing pole with equipment like mine? I make chirping noises, which bounce off the surface of the water. That helps me locate the ripples left behind by fish. I can even detect how deep they are swimming.

I then swoop down with my oversized hind feet and large, hooked claws. I know how to spear a fish with sharp canine teeth, then crush its skull. God made my cheeks out of stretchy membrane with special pouches as storage space for hauling fish home to my roost in hollowed-out trees or abandoned buildings. Sometimes I devour my fish in the air as I fly. I can eat 30 to 40 fish each night!

You might have seen me following pelicans around in the late afternoon as they skim the water for fish. I let the pelicans fish first and plunge in after whatever they miss. Sneaky, don't you think?

If I'm craving a quick snack away from the water, I'll settle for crickets, beetles, winged ants, and stinkbugs—but oh, how I love those fish!

God thought of everything when he created me—**Bulldog Fishing Bat.**

Tell a Friend

God supplies all of his creation with food as they need it. He also supplies his people with spiritual food from his Word. How does the Bible satisfy your spiritual appetite?

Read About It

"Blessed are those who are hungry and thirsty for what is right. They will be filled."—Matthew 5:6

In Leviticus chapter 11, God instructs the Israelites not to eat certain animals and insects. He called them "unclean." Bats are mentioned in verse 19.

Pray About It

Dear God, help me to hunger after your Word just like I crave my favorite foods.

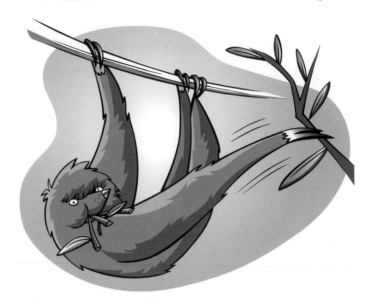

Life in the Slow Lane

I'm almost 20 years old, and have seen a lot of seasons come and go. My mother gave birth to me here in the tropical forest of Central America while hanging upside down from a tree! At birth I weighed less than a pound and measured 10 inches. Now I'm about the size of a large house cat.

Each of my hairs is grooved, which allows algae to grow into the grooves and form a nice slimy layer on my fur. Algae turns my coat green and helps me blend in with my green surroundings. My grooved hair, in turn, gives algae a place to get closer to sunlight.

My body systems run extremely slowly, so I don't need a lot of food and water. I live mostly off tasty twigs, leaves, and buds that are within reach. I am a homebody and spend most of my time hanging upside down from a tree branch. The only way I can get around on solid ground is to reach forward, grab a firm toehold, and drag my body along the ground. I wouldn't stand a chance down there with a hungry jaguar!

My stomach has many compartments to digest my favorite food—tough twigs. My teeth grow continuously because I wear them down by chewing the twigs. I also enjoy snacking on leaves, buds, fruit, and small prey.

God thought of everything when he created me—**Two-Toed Sloth.**

Tell a Friend

Have you ever had a great idea, but given up because it felt like too much work? Don't be like the Two-Toed Sloth, who just hangs around all day biding his time. Make your days count by committing each one to God and asking him what he has for you to accomplish.

Read About It

"Commit to the Lord everything you do. Then your plans will succeed." —Proverbs 16:3

In the King James Version of the Bible, Proverbs 18:9 compares a sloth to a lazy person who doesn't want to work.

Pray About It

Thank you, God, for the gift of life. Help me to pay attention to what you have for me to do.

Friends Call Me "Digger"

God planned for females of my species to have four babies at a time—every time they give birth!

My big family originally came from Mexico. Over the years, my aunts, uncles, and cousins spread throughout the southeastern United States. Other relatives live in South America. In fact, there are over 20 different types of our species in the world. Imagine what a family reunion would look like!

God knew that I would need tools for digging, so he equipped me with long, powerful claws. I use them like shovels to dig a cozy burrow underground. There I spend my days tucked away from predators. When night falls, I leave my home to forage for food.

I crave ants and termites the way you love pizza and hamburgers. Using my shovel feet, I tunnel into a termite's nest. Once I create that passageway, I lean in close and stick my snout into the hole. My long, sticky tongue lashes out and grabs a mouthful of wriggling goodies. *Yum!*

God gave me a special coat of armor to protect me from predators. The armor is made of bands of hard, bony plates. Between each band lies a flexible layer of skin, which allows me to move my legs. This special suit protects my head, shoulders, hips, and tail. To protect my soft belly, I pull in my legs and press my underside hard against the ground. Sometimes I pull my feet in and roll up in a tight ball, too.

God thought of everything when he created me—**Armadillo.**

Tell a Friend

God provides for an Armadillo's daily needs. In what ways does God provide for you and your family?

Read About It

"Give thanks no matter what happens. God wants you to thank him because you believe in Christ Jesus."—1 Thessalonians 5:18

My eyes are very sensitive to light. I only come out during cloudy weather, late afternoon, or at night.

Pray About It

Dear God, thank you for creating me and taking care of me.

Dressed for Dinner

I am a member of a species called vultures. On a rocky ledge far above the Himalayan tree line, I make my home in a nest woven of sticks. The Himalayas have been called the place where earth meets sky, and what a view I have!

I'm sure no canary! I measure nearly 3 feet long, with a wingspan of almost 10 feet. I tip the scales at about 15 pounds—as much as a Thanksgiving turkey! Although I'm strong and speedy, I don't hunt alone. Instead, I fly with a group that hovers in the air to stake out our next meal. My victim isn't hard to catch because my species feasts only on *carcasses*, which are the bodies of dead animals.

That might sound like a disgusting way to find a meal, but we play an important role in cleaning up the countryside. A group of us can pick a carcass apart in a few hours using our sharp, hooked bills. By ridding the land of carcasses, we help prevent the spread of disease. Although I often feast on animals that have died of disease, I remain healthy because God gave me a special resistance to illness.

God knows how cold the temperatures get at an elevation of two miles up, so guess what he did? He provided a long layer of soft, warm feathers that surround my neck like a warm ruffle.

God thought of everything when he created me—**Himalayan Griffon.**

Tell a Friend

The Himalayan Griffon picks apart a carcass for survival. Sometimes in the heat of anger, our words can pick someone apart, too. Spoken out of anger or jealousy, words have the power to kill someone's confidence and make them feel unloved or unlovely. Have you ever been on the receiving end of an angry outburst? How did you handle it?

Read About It

"Those who talk a lot are likely to sin. But those who control their tongues are wise."—Proverbs 10:19

Without God, many people live in fear and blame God for their problems. The Bible speaks of them as people who wander around "like food for vultures" (Job 15:23).

Pray About It

Lord, help me to choose words that help, not hurt.

More Than a Shade Tree

I've been called the tree that God planted upside down. My thick trunk ends in a wild tangle of root-like branches at the top. They look like skinny arms waving at the sky. I originated in Africa, and because of the enormous size of my trunk, experts believe that I am thousands of years old. It is hard to estimate my exact age, though, because my trunk does not have any rings to count.

If the world held a contest to find the most useful tree, I might win. My leaves are cooked as a vegetable similar to spinach. They are also used to treat insect bites and other medical conditions like asthma and kidney problems. I blossom when I am about 20 years old. Pollen from my flowers is mixed with water to make glue.

God made me useful to travelers. My flowers wilt within 24 hours and fall to the ground where their petals are eaten by birds.

My vitamin-rich fruits and seeds provide food for a weary passerby. Hollow out my huge trunk, and you can sleep inside me. In some places, my trunk is even used as a water storage tank.

If you like music, use the fiber of my bark to make a stringed instrument. It can also be used to make rope, cloth, and baskets. I'll grow new bark wherever the old bark is stripped away.

God thought of everything when he created me—**Baobab Tree.**

Tell a Friend

The Baobab Tree is a giver. In the same way, God is honored when we help those in need.

Read About It

"Anyone who is kind to poor people lends to the Lord. God will reward him for what he has done."—Proverbs 19:17

Pray About It

Lord, you have given me gifts to share with others. Help me to honor you through my actions and thoughts.

My flowers give off a musky scent and bloom only at night. The moonlight blossoms attract fruit bats, which drink the nectar and pass my pollen from flower to flower.

God Gave Me Goggles

Ideveloped in a nest that my mother dug in the backwoods near a river. There she laid a few dozen eggs, then covered the nest with leaves and other debris. The covering kept her babies-to-be warm and safe as they grew. For three months she carefully guarded her eggs—even to the point of skipping meals.

One day, the other hatchlings and I broke out of our shells and announced our arrival with high-pitched chirps. Our mother and father both sprang into action, digging to reach us. They gently rolled any unhatched eggs between their teeth and the roof of their mouths to help free the hatchlings.

In the early weeks of life, my mother carried us around in a pouch under her lower jaw. My parents worked together to protect us for about two years. During that time, they taught us how to live on our own.

I have a lizard-like shape and a rough, scaly hide. But I'm much bigger than a lizard and will grow up to 20 feet long. Unlike lizards, I do not shed my skin. As I grow larger, my skin grows with me.

My ears and nostrils close when I dive underwater. God also created a second pair of eyelids for me. These see-through eyelids drop down to cover my eyes when I dive or swim. Thanks to God's design, I can see underwater without getting murky water in my eyes. Don't you wish you had built-in swimming goggles like mine?

God thought of everything when he created me—**Nile Crocodile.**

Tell a Friend

God gave the Nile Crocodile special eyes to see underwater. When we ask Jesus into our lives, the Bible says we become a new creation. It's like gaining a new set of eyes that can help us view the world differently.

Read About It

"Anyone who believes in Christ is a new creation. The old is gone! The new has come!"—2 Corinthians 5:17

I have been known to gallop on dry land at speeds up to 29 miles per hour. If I were a car driving in your neighborhood, I might get a speeding ticket!

Pray About It

Dear God, help me to see the wonderful things you have for me in your world.

A Pesky Picnic
Party Pooper

Nobody invites me to a family campout or backyard barbecue. I spend most of my life dodging people who chase me down and swat at me. I beat my wings 165 to 200 times per second—over twice the speed of a hummingbird! Special muscles work to lift and lower my wings. A small opening in my midsection pulls in air when I flap my wings. That supplies oxygen to my tiny muscles because I don't have lungs like humans.

I am attracted to strong smells, like sweet flowers, rotting fruit, or a nice fresh pile of pig or cow manure. I don't have teeth for chewing, so a drop or two of vomit helps dissolve food into a liquid treat. I can also peel my lips back if necessary, and use the sharp, jagged edge of my mouth for scraping food in hard-to reach places. You have taste buds on your tongue, but mine are in and around my mouth, and even on my *feet*. That's right—I can taste with my tootsies!

So hold onto your hamburgers! Protect your hot dogs! I'm always on the lookout for my next meal, and trust me—you do not want me to land anywhere near your plate. I may not be welcome at your next family reunion, but I do have a purpose in life: I provide a scrumptious snack for snakes and frogs!

God thought of everything when he created me—**Housefly.**

Tell a Friend

God has a purpose for every living thing. He created you with a special plan in mind—a plan that will use your unique talents and abilities.

Read About It

"God is working in you. He wants your plans and your acts to be in keeping with his good purpose."—Philippians 2:13

I have wraparound eyes that help me sense movement nearby. My eyes work ten times faster than a human eye.

Pray About It

Lord, I want to know your special plan for my life. Help me to walk close to you as I discover it.

A Fair-Weather Forecaster

When insect experts discovered me, they called me one of the most striking insect finds of the century. I belong to a family called *Giant weta.* It's my family name, just like your last name.

I hail from New Zealand where I make myself at home in secondhand tunnels. A large beetle that doesn't live here anymore dug the home I currently live in. If I can't locate a ready-made apartment, I'll settle for a warm, dry crevice near the edge of a building. I'll also snuggle inside a hollow tree or the hollow stem of a plant.

God taught me how to protect myself. I'm covered in a scaly suit of armor, and I only enter my hollow home headfirst. My spiny hind legs block the entrance to the passage behind me so nothing can follow me inside. Smart trick, don't you think?

My antennae are twice the length of my body. Every evening before I go outside to hunt, I slowly back out of the tunnel. Sensory organs on my rear end can tell whether it's cold, warm, wet, or dry.

I only hunt at night, so if the weather sounds good I'll venture out. My favorite kind of night is warm, damp, and dark.

God thought of everything when he created me—**Giant Grasshopper.**

Tell a Friend

If weather conditions aren't perfect, the Giant Grasshopper stays inside. Some friendships change almost as often as the weather. A "fair-weather friend" is loyal only when things suit him or her. What kind of a friend are you?

Read About It

"Even a man who has many companions can be destroyed. But there is a friend who sticks closer than a brother."—Proverbs 18:24

The Bible mentions some of my hungry cousins in Psalm 78:46. "He gave their crops to the grasshoppers. He gave their food to the locusts."

Pray About It

Lord, help me to be a faithful friend—one who is kind-hearted, forgiving, and loyal—just like Jesus!

The Stinky Flying Cow

I'm a happy *folivore*—a bird who thrives on leaves. Most birds dream of their next plump meal of insects, seeds, or fruits, but if I had to choose a special birthday dinner, I'd request a pile of chewy leaves. For dessert, I'd nibble sweet berries.

I began life without feathers in a messy nest overlooking the flooded plains of Venezuela. When monkeys or snakes came near, I would dive into the waters below. There I learned to swim well and when the coast was clear, I could run back up the tree trunk to the safety of my nest again. God planned for my claws to fall off once I learned to fly.

I'm fully grown now with chestnut-brown feathers framing a bright blue face and red eyes. A crest of colorful feathers sits atop my head like a fancy hat. Sometimes I am mistaken for a pheasant, but my closest relative is the cuckoo. I am the size of a plump chicken, and I smell like cow manure. Onlookers often make fun of my clumsy movements. I've been called names like "flying cow" or even worse—"stinkbird."

Because leaves are tough to digest, I store ground-up leaves in a pouch in my throat called a crop. There they soak in bacteria to soften and prepare for digestion—much the way a cow digests grass.

God thought of everything when he created me—**Hoatzin.**

Tell a Friend

The Hoatzin is one of the oddest birds alive and has earned a strange reputation for itself. The Bible cautions us about labeling people who look different. Remember that God looks at the heart, not at how we look.

Read About It

"I do not look at the things people look at. Man looks at how someone appears on the outside. But I look at what is in the heart."—1 Samuel 16:7

I was described in science books for the first time in 1775.

Pray About It

Heavenly Father, help me to see others the way you do—from the inside out.

Watch Your Tongue!

I'm a member of a group that includes sow bugs and pill bugs. I don't live on land as they do, but in the deep waters of the Gulf of California. You won't find me sunning myself in a shoreline tide pool, either. My life is much busier than that.

I make my home inside the mouth of a fish called the Spotted Rose Snapper. I'm picky about where I live, and you won't find me accepting room and board with any other type of fish. I'm not tagging along for the ride either. I attach myself to my host's tongue and suck blood for nourishment. I suck so much blood, in fact, the snapper's tongue eventually shrivels up and dies, leaving behind a stub.

But hey, I'm not heartless! I don't desert my host in its hour of need. I stick around—literally. Using hook-like arms on my underside, I clamp onto the stub and take over the duties of a tongue. My host can count on me to help it grab food. When I'm hungry, I snack on bits of floating food.

I'm known as a parasite because I live off my Spotted Rose Snapper. Once I take over as its tongue, it's a partnership to the end!

God thought of everything when he created me—**Isopod.**

Tell a Friend

The Spotted Rose Snapper doesn't know to guard its tongue. If it did, that clingy Isopod would not have a chance! The Bible teaches about the importance of guarding our tongues, too. Do you think before you speak or say things that hurt others?

Read About It

"Anyone who is careful about what he says keeps himself out of trouble."—Proverbs 21:23

Pray About It

Lord, help me to guard my tongue, and to use it to speak words that encourage.

I'm the only known parasite that actually replaces an important body part of its host.

Homebody at Heart

The desert is the only place I have ever known. My burrow home is shaped like an upside-down U and is only three inches in diameter. At the bottom of the burrow is a cool, flat area where I rest. I only wander out at night when the temperatures are cooler.

I measure 10 inches from head to tail, but my bushy tail is longer than my body. God knew I would need to spring across the loose, soft sand of my home in the southwestern United States. He designed my large, hairy-soled back feet bigger than my two front feet. I have four toes on each hind foot, while many of my cousins have five. My shorter front feet have strong claws, which are perfect for digging my deep burrow.

I have long puzzled scientists for several reasons. For one thing, I don't sweat or pant to keep my body cool like other animals. Water is scarce here in the desert, but guess what? My body changes dry seeds into liquid nourishment! Kidneys usually need lots of water to rid the body of waste, but my Maker gave me special kidneys. They work just fine without water. I'm not like a camel, which stores water in its body for future use. I don't store a single drop of water, and yet, experiments have shown that my body has as much water content as other animals!

God thought of everything when he created me—**Kangaroo Rat.**

Tell a Friend

The Kangaroo Rat does not venture too far from home. He has found contentment in familiar surroundings. What does home mean to you?

Read About It

"You gain a lot when you live a godly life. But you must be happy with what you have. We didn't bring anything into the world. We can't take anything out of it. If we have food and clothing, we will be happy with that."—1 Timothy 6:6-8

If a rattlesnake slithers near, I turn and kick sand into its face.

Pray About It

Lord, I am grateful that you take care of all my needs. Thank you for preparing an eternal home in Heaven that will be mine someday.

Behold, the Beached Blob

I'm a jelly-like sea animal with a body that resembles a clear plastic bag. Filled with gas, I float on the surface of the water, pushed along by the waves and wind. Members of my family live in the warm waters of the world. People have reported seeing up to 1,000 of us floating together!

I am blue, but some of us are shades of pink, too. We grow anywhere from 3 to 12 inches.

My underside contains coiled tentacles that can grow up to 165 feet long! I use my tentacles to capture prey: crayfish, plankton, and small fish. I grab them and paralyze them with a sting. My sting is like a shot of poison and is said to be almost as powerful as the venom of a cobra!

Since I spend my life floating, I have no way of controlling where I end up. God knew I would need direction in my life, so he designed a special body part called a crest. My crest looks like a sail. The wind catches my crest and floats me from place to place. When waves knock me around, I use my muscles to pull myself back up again.

To keep my body from drying out, I dip my crest in the water often. Sometimes accidents happen, and strong winds push some of us ashore.

God thought of everything when he created me—**Portuguese Man-of-War.**

Tell a Friend

God controls the direction of the winds that push the Portuguese Man-of–War along. His Word gives us direction for our lives, too.

Read About It

"'I know the plans I have for you,' announces the Lord. 'I want you to enjoy success. I do not plan to harm you. I will give you hope for the years to come.'"—Jeremiah 29:11

If you ever spot me washed up on a beach, do not touch me! I may look dead, but I am still able to give a painful, poisonous sting.

Pray About It

Lord, help me to listen to your voice and to hear the plans you have for my life.

I Love a Good Hug!

I'll never win a trophy for having a friendly personality. Some even call me the bully of the jungle. But can I help that I'm hungry all the time?

My appetite has grown tremendously since my baby days when I measured a wee 24 inches. At 22 feet long and 550 pounds, it takes a lot to satisfy me now! I'd much rather feast on a deer than a mouse, but I'll eat whatever is available if I'm hungry. Watch out, turtles! Watch out, iguanas! You're listed on my menu, too.

I have eyes on top of my head, which keeps me alert for my next meal. When a tasty treat wanders my way, I don't mess around. I coil my powerful body around my victim and give it a gigantic hug until it quits breathing. God created me with a special jaw that unhinges. It allows me to open my mouth w-i-d-e and eat animals that would normally be too large to swallow.

On a sunny day, I'll sometimes slither to the water's edge and rest in the grass awhile. I wish God had not made me taste so good though. Bloodsucking ticks find me whenever I settle down for a riverside nap. They march across my yellow and black back like soldiers in a parade. *Ouch!*

God thought of everything when he made me—**Anaconda.**

Tell a Friend

God created each Anaconda to be unique. How are you and your best friend different? In what ways are you alike?

Read About It

"God said, 'Let the land produce all kinds of living creatures. Let there be livestock, and creatures that move along the ground, and wild animals. Let there be all kinds of them.' And that's exactly what happened."—Genesis 1:24

Pray About It

Thanks for fitting the world together with so many unique parts, Lord.

I don't lay eggs; instead, I give birth to up to 100 wriggling, slithering babies at a time. Each of my babies has a different marking on the underside of its tail, just as humans have a different fingerprint.

Picnic in the Pond

Would you be able to go a whole year without eating? I can—if I have to. As I feed on turtles, frogs, and certain insects, my body swells nearly five times its normal size. Most days, you'll find me at the bottom of a pond feasting on things that have died there. I look like a flattened worm and can move through the water like a snake.

God gave me a suction-cup mouth and suction cups on my tail. If I want to travel on the surface of the water, I attach my mouth to a log or rock, push forward, and then use my tail suckers in the same way. I look like a bicycle wheel rolling slowly along. I have strong jaws and sharp mouthparts to pierce the skin of my prey. My saliva contains a special painkiller and a chemical that prevents my victim's blood from clotting and forming a scab. I feast on a meal of blood and other body fluids.

In certain cases, doctors have used members of my family to help certain types of patients. When a badly-burned person needs a skin graft, for example, a blood-sucking cousin of mine is able to help rid the damaged area of excess blood. This causes blood to flow normally until new blood vessels, called capillaries, can take over.

Patients heal more quickly thanks to my busy cousin.

God thought of everything when he created me—**Leech.**

Tell a Friend

Problems are like Leeches. They make us worry day and night. Worry has the power to suck our energy and enthusiasm, but there's good news: God is ever near, ready to rescue us from worry.

Read About It

"I tell you, do not worry . . . But put God's kingdom first. Do what he wants you to do."—Matthew 6:25, 33

Pray About It

Lord, when worry attaches itself to me, remind me that you are as close as a prayer.

Some members of my family live in the nasal passages of horses, but I prefer the bottom of a murky pond.

Ready . . . Set . . . Fire Away!

Have you ever visited Java? Java is an island in Indonesia. Its mountains are home to my family and me. If you see a furry little creature with a beautiful white stripe running the length of its back, that's me! I may not be very big, but don't let my short, stocky appearance fool you. God equipped me with a smart way to protect myself from pushy predators. If any enemy startles or threatens my safety, I can make my body go completely limp and play dead. How's that for a slick trick? Or, depending on my mood, I can turn around, lift my short furry tail, and spray a toxic, oily green substance. I'm one of the best shots around and can score a direct hit from over three feet away.

I sometimes don't notice when an enemy lurks nearby. The Javan Hawk-Eagle, for example, would love to swoop down and snatch me up for a tasty lunch. If I sense him circling overhead, I don't waste time figuring out what to do. I just trot off in the opposite direction to hide until he's gone.

Chances are slim that you'll ever bump into me. I only come out at night. Daylight hours find me resting inside my burrow. I dig my burrow with my sharp claws. At the bottom lies a roomy chamber, big enough for a bed. I make my bed from leaves, twigs, and other plant litter. My friend the porcupine likes my burrow so much, he sometimes curls up for a nap with me. He respects my stinky weapon, and I respect his prickly needles. Humans call ours an unusual friendship

God thought of everything when he created me—**Stink Badger.**

Tell a Friend

God taught the Stink Badger how to handle its enemies. Have you ever felt cornered by someone who treated you unkindly? Read today's verse and write it in you own words.

Read About It

"Instead, worship me. I will save you from the powerful hand of all your enemies."—2 Kings 17:39

I'm a Bible star! Psalm 104:18 speaks of the animals that live on cliffs, including badgers.

Pray About It

You have the answer to every problem, Lord. Thank you for loving and watching over me!

Ready or Not—
Here I Come!

Think of your favorite snack and multiply it by 30,000. That's how many ants and termites I can eat in a single day. Before I learned to hunt, I depended on my mother for everything. Even though I could move around in a slow gallop at four weeks after birth, I spent almost a year clinging to my mother's back. She protected me from big wild cats like jaguars and pumas.

God designed my head in a tube shape with a long, slender snout. He equipped me with sharp claws to rip open ant nests. Just as you use your tongue to lick ice-cream cones, I use mine for locating insects inside their nests. God knew how deep some of these termite and ant mounds can be, so he gave me a two-foot-long tongue! Once I tear into a tall termite or ant mound, my "super tongue" flits in and out of the nest so fast, insects can't escape.

I live alone in the grasslands of South America. All day long I search for food, and my sharp sense of smell and hearing help me to locate insects quickly.

Of course, I can't hunt all the time. At night, I dig a little hollow in the soft soil and curl up to sleep. Sometimes I use the deserted burrow of another animal, too. My long, bushy tail helps keep me warm like a built-in blanket.

God thought of everything when he created me—**Giant Anteater.**

Tell a Friend

God equipped the Giant Anteater with an extra-long tongue for hunting. What body parts do you most appreciate? Thank God for equipping you with exactly what you need.

Read About It

"How you made me is amazing and wonderful. I praise you for that. What you have done is wonderful. I know that very well."
—Psalm 139:14

I am the largest and best-known species of ant-eating animals. Covered with gray, bristly hair, I can grow over six feet long. My tail alone measures three feet!

Pray About It

Lord, thank you for equipping me with all that I need to live. Help me to use my body in a way that pleases you.

King of the Hoppers

If you think all frogs look the same, think again. God designed me different from all others. My body measures over one foot across. I am bigger than a piece of toast, bigger than your hand, and way bigger than most books about frogs. Stretch my legs out straight and I measure almost three feet long from nose to toe!

I live in sparkling mountain streams in Cameroon, a country located in west central Africa. Other members of my family live in swift-moving rivers that wind through the dense rain forest of Cameroon and Equatorial Guinea. I am a shy frog, plus you won't catch me croaking on warm summer nights because I was born without a voice sac.

I don't have a voice, but I do have a gigantic hop! If you were to enter me in a frog jumping contest, guess who would win?

Scientists are puzzled by my size. For one thing, my mother's eggs are the same as any other frog's eggs. And I was never bigger than the other tadpoles. *Hmmmm . . .* God must have planned for me to be a giant among my species! Who am I to argue with my Creator?

God thought of everything when he created me—**Goliath Frog.**

Tell a Friend

The Bible refers to God as our potter. Every member of creation is a one-of-a-kind handiwork. God takes delight in his work. Have you thanked him lately for making you just as you are?

Read About It

"Lord, you are our Father. We are the clay. You are the potter. Your hands made all of us."—Isaiah 64:8

Pray About It

Lord, your world is filled with unusual creatures. I am unusual too—in a good way! Thank you for making me one-of-a-kind.

Another Goliath is mentioned in the Bible, but he isn't a frog. Read all about this gigantic man in 1 Samuel 17.

Following the Crowd

Long before I was able to hop or fly, I grew inside an egg pod. My egg was the size of a grain of rice. A frothy mixture covered me until I hatched into a tiny nymph. Several changes and about two months later, I became an adult.

I live in a dry area of northern Africa. Some members of my family travel alone at night, but I am a species that migrates from place to place. A *plague* happens when billions of us band together to cover a wide area of land. A group of us is called a swarm and can spread quickly into as many as 60 countries, eating every plant in our path.

I was designed for movement. God gave me the ability to jump 10 times my body length in one leap! A waxy layer covers my entire body preventing moisture from evaporating in the hot, dry climate where I live. He taught me how to follow the wind currents. My swarm knows when to leave and how to stay on course. We progress at about 12 miles per hour and can travel as far as 80 miles per day.

One report claims that in 1950, swarms of us were tracked from the Arabian Peninsula to the west coast of Africa in less than two months. That's over 3,000 miles!

God thought of everything when he created me—**Desert Locust.**

Tell a Friend

The Desert Locust spends a lifetime following the crowd. If the swarm turns left, it turns left. When the group speeds up, it speeds up. Do you follow a crowd, like the locust, and let friends make all your decisions? Be very careful who you follow and where they lead you.

Read About It

"Teach me to do what you want, because you are my God. May your good Spirit lead me on a level path."—Psalm 143:10

The Bible is filled with verses about me. Read Exodus 10 to see what happened when Pharaoh refused to free the Israelites from slavery in Egypt.

Pray About It

Dear Lord, help me to remember that following you is always the best course.

Brainy and Brawny— That's Me!

I was hatched inside a rocky den, six weeks after my mother hung a clump of eggs there. She watched over me while I developed inside the egg, squirting my shell with water and guarding it against predators. My family has over 150 species. Some grow only as big as a jelly bean. The biggest weighs over 550 pounds and measures almost 23 feet across!

I've been called the most mysterious and smartest creature in the ocean. God gave me an amazing brain and eight busy arms, called tentacles. Researchers have spent years studying my movements and habits, trying to understand why I'm so smart. Scientists know that my brain controls vision and movement. For example, if my next meal swims by, my brain jumps into high gear. It tells my arms which direction to target and how fast to move.

Researchers also now believe that each of my eight arms know what the other is doing—just as your left hand knows what your right hand is up to. They hope to use the results of their research to create a robotic arm that will help people who have lost an arm in an accident. The arm would be designed much the way my tentacles are, with nerve centers that move when their brain tells it to. Can you blame me for bragging about being chosen for this special project?

God thought of everything when he created me—**Octopus.**

Tell a Friend

God made each of us brainy in a different way. He gave us abilities and talents to use for good. Think of a time when you felt bigheaded and acted like a braggart. How did others react to that?

Read About It

"If you really want to become wise, you must begin by having respect for the Lord. To know the Holy One is to gain understanding."
—Proverbs 9:10

My mother lays more than 100,000 eggs!

Pray About It

Dear Lord, thank you for loving me so. Give me a heart of wisdom, so I can please you in all I do.

A Skinny, Toothless Wonder

I live in muddy canals, swamps, and slow-flowing rivers like the Amazon. If you could peer down into my murky brown home, you'd find me sitting motionless in the mud, waiting to snatch an earthworm, minnow, or other small water creature. Covered with tiny sensory hairs, my star-shaped fingers help me locate food quickly.

If a small fish tries to sneak by, my mouth turns into a vacuum cleaner. I don't have a tongue or teeth, but God taught me know to expand my body, lunge forward, and suck in a passing fish. If the fish is too large, I use my front legs to turn it around until I can swallow it whole. I am able to stay underwater for up to an hour at a time.

I announce my territory by making clicking noises. If an enemy or another toad ventures too close, my clicking turns frantic, and I will fight to protect my territory. My back legs are powerful, allowing me to push through the water at high speeds.

When I'm not hunting, I like to float on the warm surface of the water. Although I'm surrounded by liquid, I don't ever drink water. Instead, my skin acts as a sponge, absorbing water into my body.

God thought of everything when he created me—**Surinam Toad.**

Tell a Friend

The Surinam Toad is surrounded by water, yet never drinks any of it. In the same way, our lives are surrounded by choices—both good and bad. The Bible helps us make wise choices. It is a special guidebook—a gift from God. Have you thanked him for it lately?

Read About It

"Anyone who gets wisdom loves himself. Anyone who values understanding succeeds."—Proverbs 19:8

Pray About It

Sometimes I feel confused, Lord, and don't know which way to turn. Thank you for providing clear instructions in your Word.

I'm a toad, but I don't look much like one. Rectangular with a flat-topped head, I am often mistaken for a leaf floating in the water.

51

An Unlikely Friendship

Whoever heard of a friendship between ants and butterflies? Well, I have! I belong to a family of butterflies who depend on red ants for survival. God planned for us to become friends who cooperate.

During my caterpillar stage, I sent a signal to red ants, telling them it was time for them to adopt me. An ant showed up within minutes and began tapping my body with its antennae. Ordinary ants would have eaten me for lunch, but not the red ant! It waited for me to release a droplet of sweet, honey-like nectar from my special nectary organ. The nectar is an important part of the ant's diet.

After the ant had eaten its fill, I flattened my body to make it easy for it to carry me to its nest. There it placed me in a special room where the ant larvae live. Worker ants treated me just like one of the family. They fed me so well, my body weight increased 100 times in one month!

I stayed with the ants throughout the fall, winter, and spring months, changing from caterpillar to pupa inside my cocoon. After hatching, I had to work my way through that ant-filled nest to an exit. Some ants didn't want me to leave, though! God protected me by covering my body with a hair-like armor of loose scales. When an ant tried to bite me, all it got was a mouthful of scales.

God thought of everything when he created me—**Alcon Blue Butterfly.**

Tell a Friend

God creates friendships when we least expect them. He uses creatures like ants and butterflies to teach us how to get along with one another. How did you and your best friend meet? Share why your friendship is so special.

Read About It

"Carry each other's heavy loads. If you do, you will give the law of Christ its full meaning."—Galatians 6:2

Pray About It

Lord, thank you for giving me faithful friends who care about me.

In my caterpillar form, I will die unless I am adopted into a nest of ants.

53

Beware of Swinging Doors!

Most snakes devour their victims by opening their mouths as wide as possible and working each side slowly around and over their prey.

I have my own way of swallowing my prey. Because of my size, I avoid antelopes and rats in favor of ants. At seven inches long, and as thick as a strand of spaghetti, I am the shortest snake in the world.

God knew that my craving for ants would take me inside narrow passageways. A normal snake would not be able to spread its mouth open wide down there, but my Creator designed a special lower jaw that allows me to maneuver in tight spots and eat quickly.

It is equipped with six sets of teeth. Built with three joints—at the chin, and at either side—the jaw divides in the middle, yet both sides work together. Each half bends in, then out, and has been compared to a set of swinging doors. They swing open, then close quickly, raking ants and larvae into my mouth. Researchers watched me dropping and retrieving my jaw flaps at the rate of four times per second.

The faster I eat, the faster I can exit the nest before the ants turn on me. If a band of angry ants were to corner me, I wouldn't stand a chance because of my size.

God thought of everything when he created me—**Texas Threadsnake.**

Tell a Friend

The Threadsnake's jaw has been compared to swinging doors. That's a good way to describe the mouth of a person who gossips, too. Out goes the rumor; in comes the feedback. Once spoken, words cannot be taken back. "Think before you speak" is a good motto to live by.

Read About It

"With our tongues we praise our Lord and Father. With our tongues we call down curses on people. We do it even though they have been created to be like God. Praise and cursing come out of the same mouth."—James 3:9, 10

While most snakes take hours to consume their victim, I can eat an entire meal in seconds!

Pray About It

Heavenly Father, help me to be aware of the weight of my words, and that others are affected by what I say.

Humongously Hungry

Have you noticed a small mouse-like critter scampering around your backyard or garden? Probably not, since I usually only come out at night. I live in a burrow underground, or beneath a pile of leaves or bark. Sometimes I even borrow a bedroom in the tunnel of a mouse or mole.

Members of my species vary in size from two to six inches, but don't let our small bodies fool you. Our appetites are humongous! God gave us the fastest metabolic rate of any animal. Every body function, from digestion to breathing, is speedy. For example, my heart beats 700 times a minute, and I breathe 10 times more often than you do!

Tiny mammals like me need lots of energy just to stay warm. I get my energy from eating, so I am forever on the lookout for food. I snack all day long on earthworms, berries, snails, and spiders. If I'm desperate, I'll sneak food from your pet's dish, too. I eat up to twice my body weight in food every single day!

My vision is not the best, but I have a keen sense of hearing, smell, and touch. My small size doesn't discourage me from making a meal of animals twice my size, either. How does a little guy like me protect himself? Easy! I smell like rotting garlic, so hungry animals don't venture too close.

God thought of everything when he created me—**Shrew.**

Tell a Friend

God gave the Shrew a gigantic appetite for food. God's Word is often referred to as "food." When we take time to read the Bible, it makes us hungry for more.

Read About It

"Your words are very sweet to my taste! They are sweeter than honey to me."—Psalm 119:103

A 100-pound person would have to eat 200 pounds of food a day to keep up with my appetite.

Pray About It

Lord, I want to know you better. Give me a hunger to learn more about you.

Stop 'n' Go Fish

My mother gave birth to me one autumn in Lake Baikal, Siberia. Females of my species don't lay eggs; their offspring are live, fully-developed little fish, called fries. I knew how to swim immediately after birth.

My family doesn't travel in large schools. From early on, I lived a solitary life. I also learned to adjust to the pressure of life at 700 to 1,600 feet deep. When I journey down in the water, I stop to let my body adjust to the changing water pressure and temperature. Every night I make a trip up to the water's surface, stopping along the way when needed. I return to the depths in the morning.

My body is extremely sensitive to any temperature change. To me the perfect water temperature is 41 degrees. If the water warms up to 50 degrees, I could die.

I don't have scales like other fish, and my body is made of about 30 percent oil, rich in vitamin A. Although I am not fit for eating, my flesh is in demand for other purposes. Long ago, members of my species were picked up on the beaches after a big storm. The fat was melted and used in treatments for arthritis, heart disease, and healing wounds—all practices that have made me a sought-after fish even today. Native Siberians still use my fat for their oil lamps and for medicine.

God thought of everything when he created me—**Golomyanka.**

Tell a Friend

The Golomyanka lives with extreme pressure, but God taught it when to stop and rest. Are you feeling pressured by a problem or a busy schedule? God has a solution in the verse below.

Read About It

"Turn all your worries over to him. He cares about you."—1 Peter 5:7

My species is the most plentiful fish in Lake Baikal. We account for about 150,000 tons of fish.

Pray About It

Dear God, when life gets hectic, help me to stop everything and turn to you for help.

Guess What's on the Menu

At first glance, you might think I'm just a filthy, good-for-nothing insect. After all, I survive by feeding on the dung from large plant-eating mammals, such as zebras, cows, kangaroos, and elephants.

You might have to look closely to spot me. I have an excellent sense of smell, which helps me locate fresh piles of dung. Male insects of my species are so competitive, an entire dung pad can disappear within three hours! They try to impress future mates by creating the fanciest ball of dung. How romantic is that?

Some species in my family live underground in tunnels. The females dig the tunnels, and lay eggs in dung that is shoved down the tunnel by male beetles. The babies, called grubs, are born into a ready-made cafeteria. *Yum!*

Males spend their days sculpting dung balls to roll into the underground chamber. Some species prefer to set up housekeeping in a nice fresh pile of waste rather than underground. That's where I live—in a big pile of poop. I lay eggs there, and my babies are born into a warm, smelly home.

Dung supplies certain bacteria and other nutrients that I need to survive. Dung also attracts extra treats—flies! God gave me a powerful set of jaws for tearing open old, dried heaps of dung and munching crunchy flies. I have a special purpose in life—to rid the countryside of dung, kill flies, and enrich the soil.

God thought of everything when he created me—**Dung Beetle.**

Tell a Friend

Our size doesn't matter. Our age doesn't matter. God made each of us with a special purpose in mind—like the Dung Beetle.

Read About It

"Work at everything you do with all your heart."—Colossians 3:23

Pray About It

I want to know the plan you have for my life, Lord. Help me to hear and obey your voice.

In the Old Testament we read about a fire that burned the city gates of Jerusalem. One of the gates was called Dung Gate. Read in Nehemiah 2:13 about a man named Nehemiah, whose job it was to inspect the gates.

Walkin' on Water

My mother laid a clutch of four eggs in a damp nest in South Africa. Four days in a row, at around 7 AM, she would lay an egg. One of those glossy brown eggs belonged to me!

My father took care of me long before I was born. He guarded the nest for about 25 days. On bright, sunny days, he would check to make sure the eggs stayed a perfect temperature. If he found the eggs too warm, he would move them into the shade; too cool, and he'd sit on them until their temperature increased.

Shortly after I hatched, my father tucked the other three hatchlings and me under his wings. He kept us warm and dry, carrying us around until we were a couple of weeks old.

My claim to fame is my toes. I have the longest toes of any bird, and they help me get a firm grip on floating water plants.

When I land on water, I keep my wings raised slightly and I swoop in like a water plane. Scientists have studied my flying and landing style and noticed that I never raise my wings when landing on dry land. God taught me to raise my wings for balance only when I land on water. Otherwise, I would sink.

God thought of everything when he created me—**African Jacana.**

Tell a Friend

The African Jacana's father watched over it long before it hatched, but we have a heavenly Father who knew us personally—and loved us—long before we drew our first breath.

Read About It

"None of my bones was hidden from you when you made me inside my mother's body. That place was as dark as the deepest parts of the earth. When you were putting me together there, your eyes saw my body even before it was formed."—Psalm 139:15, 16

God created the eggshell in which I developed with special pores to rid itself of excess moisture. He knew that I'd need a way to stay dry in the wet surroundings of the African floodplain.

Pray About It

Heavenly Father, thank you for watching over me before I was born, and all the days of my life!

Bloomin' and Fumin'

Nobody makes a vase big enough to hold me. I am the biggest flower in the whole world! My petals grow to one-and-a-half feet long and one inch thick! I grow on the island of Sumatra in Indonesia.

Before my life began, rodents and small mammals nibbled at the flowers of one of my relatives, scattering its seeds across the vast forest floor. One of those seeds germinated in the root or stem of a thick, sturdy vine that snakes across the floor of tropical forests. The seed absorbed nutrients directly from the vine, but did not grow leaves like most plants.

After about 18 months, something peculiar happened. A small brown bud appeared. The bud took another 18 months to reach maturity. God provided the exact amount of water it needed to bloom. Too much or too little water will prevent me from blossoming. A successful bloom began when I fanned open my five or six red, blotchy petals.

You will not have to wait in a long line to smell my blossoms —guaranteed! Sometimes referred to as a "corpse flower," I send out a sickening stench like rotting meat, which attracts carrion flies—a type of fly that usually shows up to feast on dead flesh.

God thought of everything when he created me—**Rafflesia Arnoldi.**

Tell a Friend

The Bible speaks of another kind of fragrance and says that we can have that same sweet smell, too. When we live in a way that pleases God, our lives reflect his love to others.

Read About It

"You are the children that God dearly loves. So be just like him. Lead a life of love, just as Christ did. He loved us. He gave himself up for us. He was a sweet-smelling offering and sacrifice to God." —Ephesians 5:1, 2

Once it blooms, my flower only lasts for three to five days before it starts to rot.

Pray About It

Thank you, Jesus, for offering up your life as a sweet-smelling sacrifice. Help others to see that you make a difference in my life.

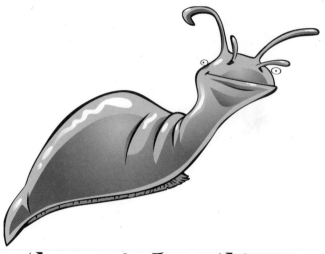

Sluggish, Slimy, and Special

You will not find me sunning myself on a hot rock, or slithering around the base of a cactus. I live only on the damp, foggy forest floor of the west coast of the United States. Small holes on the side of my head help me breathe in that cool, damp air. *Ahhhh!*

I might be sluggish, but I'm certainly not lazy! I spend my whole life cleaning the forest floor. My droppings contain a high percentage of nitrogen—something the gigantic redwood trees need to survive. I never, ever eat any part of a redwood tree. However, I will chomp away on any plant that competes with the towering redwood. I need the redwood forest, and it needs me!

God blessed me with two sets of antennae. The longer set allows me to watch where I'm going. The shorter set is for smell. If my antennae are broken off, they will grow back in two days!

In such quiet, peaceful surroundings, you'd think I'd be left alone. But no—predators like snakes, ducks, salamanders, and foxes keep me on my toes. Well, they would if I actually *had* toes! Instead of toes, I have a special muscle on the bottom of my body, called a foot. It helps me belly crawl through the forest. When an enemy threatens me, I cover myself in a thick layer of slime. That shuts down their appetite in a hurry.

God thought of everything when he created me—**Banana Slug.**

Tell a Friend

The Banana Slug uses slime as a protective covering. We do not have to fear when trouble comes our way. God promises to cover us like a blanket.

Read About It

"You are my place of safety. You are like a shield that keeps me safe. I have put my hope in your word."—Psalm 119:114

As I slither along, I mark the path with my scent so I can find my way home after dark. I also use a slime trail to find fellow slugs.

Pray About It

God, it is amazing to see how you protect even a slimy slug. Thank you for protecting me with your powerful Word—the Bible.

Bird with a Crash Helmet

If I were a driver in your neighborhood, I would receive a speeding ticket. I have been clocked at cruising speeds between 40 and 68 miles per hour. I am the fastest bird on record. Imagine that—me, the speediest bird in the whole world. But who's bragging?

I am easy to identify from a distance. A black cap of feathers hugs my head like a crash helmet—a perfect outfit for a bird with my reputation, don't you think? A mustache-shaped design of dark feathers decorates my beak.

I'm a speedy flier, but I took my time choosing a mate. My mate and I will live together our entire lives—about 15 years. Our nest sits on a tall cliff overlooking a river. If we had not been able to find a safe location for our nest, we would have chosen the top of a tall building in the middle of a busy city.

God gave me quick reactions and a keen eye to spot prey from a long way off. I am able to identify ducks, pheasants, blackbirds, and pigeons from five miles away! I dive full speed ahead in a deep plunge, catching them off guard. The sheer speed of our impact usually kills them instantly. I then swoop below a falling bird, and grab it with my long, fierce claws, called talons. My talons are sharp, which helps me hang onto my catch during my flight home.

God thought of everything when he created me—**Peregrine Falcon.**

Tell a Friend

When problems swoop down to grab you, are you easily thrown off course? Share how you handled a recent problem with God's help.

Read About It

"The Lord is a place of safety for those who have been beaten down. He keeps them safe in times of trouble."—Psalm 9:9

Pray About It

I am never outside your reach, Lord. Thank you for always watching over me.

Even though I have excellent vision, the Bible names one thing I cannot see. Read Job 28:1-7.

A Super Stretchy Neck

Why does a turtle cross the road? To get to the other side—of course! And if it happens to be spring or summer, a turtle might be looking for a spot in which to lay its eggs. I don't nest during those seasons, though. I'm different from most turtles. I lay my eggs in the cooler months and spend the winter buried underground.

You will recognize me by a pattern of yellow lines against my green shell. My head, extra-long neck, hind legs, and tail are covered with yellow stripes, too. I live in swampy areas, ponds, ditches, or small lakes. Sometimes I travel over land to hardwood forests. My favorite snack here in the swamps and ponds of Florida is crayfish.

When I was born, I measured only one inch across—about the size of a small walnut. I grew to 10 inches, but some of my cousins only reach six to seven inches. God gave me the longest neck of any turtle! My neck helps me capture small animals. Stretched to its full length, it looks like the neck of a chicken.

God thought of everything when he created me—**Chicken Turtle.**

Tell a Friend

If the Chicken Turtle never stuck its neck out, it would have to settle for eating crayfish the rest of its days. It would not be able to reach anything bigger than that. If fear prevents us from trying something new, it is often said that we are "afraid to stick our neck out." What about you? Is fear keeping you from doing something big?

Read About It

"Be strong and brave. Do not be terrified. Do not lose hope. I am the Lord your God. I will be with you everywhere you go."—Joshua 1:9

Pray About It

Lord, help me to trust you for each step and to "stick my neck out" courageously.

If you ever see me crossing a road and want to help, approach me with caution. I'm timid, and if you startle me, I might bite.

Itsy-Bitsy Spider—Not!

You won't find me tiptoeing daintily across a web because . . . *I'm bigger than a dinner plate!* If you guessed that I am the world's biggest spider, you're right. I'm covered in blondish-brown hair, and I'm related to the tarantula. My home is a burrow in the damp marshy area of a South American jungle.

A critter my size has a gigantic appetite. I've heard a report that I eat birds, but trust me—it rarely happens. Birds are too hard for me to catch! My favorite potluck consists of frogs, small snakes, lizards, beetles, and bats. I sneak up on my prey, pounce on them, and then bite them with poison-filled fangs. My method of attack has been compared to that of large jungle cats.

When I am disturbed, I let loose with a hissing noise that can be heard 15 feet away! I don't have a voice box like you, though; I make noise by rubbing my bristly legs together.

I usually save my hisses for intruders that are bigger than me, including humans.

If my hissing doesn't scare you into retreating, I have a special hair trick. God gave me the ability to shoot tiny barbed hairs into the air. Those sharp, bristly hairs will damage lungs, eyes, and skin. Hey, it's my only way of protecting myself against the giants of the world.

God thought of everything when he created me—**Goliath Bird-Eating Spider.**

Tell a Friend

The Goliath Bird-Eating Spider is known for its quick attack. Words are sometimes like that, too—quick and hurtful. God provides self-control at just the right moment, though, when we call on him.

Read About It

"A man who is wise says gracious things. But a foolish person is destroyed by what his own lips speak."—Ecclesiastes 10:12

Some South Americans eat tarantulas as a good source of protein!

Pray About It

Lord, help me to think before I speak and to treat others the way I would want to be treated.

Hide-and-Seek Hunter

What's greenish yellow with a wide dark band across its abdomen? Me, of course! I'm a sneaky bug—a skilled hunter who uses surprise to get what I want. I hide on clusters of flowers that match my colors perfectly. I'm greenish yellow, and I blend right in with a plant called goldenrod. Goldenrod flowers make a perfect hiding place for a hungry critter like me.

God fashioned special front legs for hunting. I wait on a flower for a suitable meal, such as a butterfly, bee, or wasp. The middle section of my front legs, called the femur, is thicker than the rest of my leg. Strong muscles work to control a claw-like section below. I can hold onto a fly twice my weight!

God knew that I wouldn't be able to hold onto a wriggly insect forever, so he came up with a quick solution: a thin beak that folds up under my head when not in use. It works like a needle, injecting a poisonous fluid into my victim. The fluid paralyzes it and starts to dissolve its insides. I then use my beak as a drinking straw to suck up the tasty liquid.

I might sound like an insect to avoid, but gardeners think highly of me. I help keep the population of aphids, scales, and other plant-eating bugs down.

God thought of everything when he created me—**Ambush Bug.**

Tell a Friend

Friends do not ambush each other! They do not wait for opportunities to attack unfairly. When problems come up in a friendship, handle it the way Jesus would—fairly and with kindness.

Read About It

"You are God's chosen people. You are holy and dearly loved. So put on tender mercy and kindness as if they were your clothes." —Colossians 3:12

The Bible talks about a different kind of ambush. Read Psalm 64 to learn how God protects those who trust him.

Pray About It

Dear God, show me how to love others the way you do. Thank you for your mercy and kindness toward me.

A Melon-Eating
Lawn Mower

I'm a large rodent, just like a guinea pig or a mouse, except I bet you'll never run into a 140-pound guinea pig or mouse! My scientific name, *Hydrochoerus hydrochaerus*, means "water pig." I measure over four feet long and two feet tall, and live in a family of about 20 members called a troop.

We spend cool nights searching for food. We are herbivores, which means we only eat plants. Give me a salad of grasses, roots, and bark, topped off with a dessert of melons and I'm one happy herbivore. I never sleep for long; I prefer naps all through the day. I will live to a ripe old age of eight to ten years, as long as jaguars and crocodiles don't turn me into breakfast!

I am skilled at living both in and out of water. God designed my head with small eyes and nostrils on top, similar to an alligator. My front legs are shorter than my hind legs, with webbed toes. The design of my legs helps me to paddle water or hurry across the bottom of the swamp in a running motion.

The South American Indians refer to me as Master of Grasses because I can turn an empty-looking field into a feast. Can you imagine the fun I'd have mowing your lawn?

God thought of everything when he created me—**Capybara.**

Tell a Friend

The Capybara is a master at "mowing" a field. What types of things do you do well? Have you considered how God can use your skills? Share your dream with a trusted companion and pray together.

Read About It

"Find your delight in the Lord. Then he will give you everything your heart really wants."—Psalm 37:4

Pray About It

Lord, thank you for listening to my hopes and dreams. Help me to use the skills and abilities you have given me.

I am a social animal that communicates by whistling and barking.

I've Got My Eye on You!

I'm slower than a cricket, and I'm not the most skilled hunter in the insect world. My eyesight is poor, and I grope around in the darkness—hardly an insect to raise hairs on the back of your neck.

At three inches long I might look like a scorpion off some old cowboy movie, but I am a pussycat compared to my poisonous cousin. I'm a member of a species called whip scorpions, because of my whip-like tail. I have strong pincers, which I use to shred my victim and transfer its flesh to my mouth. I can deliver a painful pinch, too, if they don't hold still! At the base of my tail lie a couple of glands where a vinegar-scented spray is produced. The acid spray can burn or sting anyone who tries to mess with me.

I am commonly found in desert areas of the southwestern United States. I sometimes venture into grasslands, pine forests, and mountain regions, too. I spend much of my time burrowed under logs and rocks. I keep a close eye on my surroundings. In fact, God gave me eight eyes—two in the middle, and three on each side of my head! I hide by day and hunt by night. Darkness does not pose a problem because I have two long feelers that are constantly on guard. I use my feelers to sense vibrations in the area.

God thought of everything when he created me—**Giant Vinegaroon.**

Tell a Friend

Looks can be deceiving, and the Giant Vinegaroon is not as harmful as it looks. God wants us to look inside a person, not at how they dress or where they live. After all, that's how God treats each of us.

Read About It

"I do not look at the things people look at. Man looks at how someone appears on the outside. But I look at what is in the heart."
—1 Samuel 16:7

A railroad camp in early-day Texas was named after me. When the railroads pushed further west, Vinegaroon was soon deserted.

Pray About It

Thank you for seeing me for who I can become in your sight, Lord—not how I look. Remind me of that whenever I meet someone new.

Cool, Calm, and Striped

I am known for my beautiful striped coat. Certain members of my large family are striped from head to toe, but not me. My striped pattern ends a ways down my sides where my belly begins. My belly is snow-white. I have long ears and a large, square flap of skin under my throat, called a dewlap.

During colder months, I seek shelter in caves or wooded ravines. The rest of the year I live in mountain grasslands at an elevation of around 6,500 feet. During warmer months, you can find me grazing in the rugged country east of the Namid Desert in Africa.

God knew that I'd need an efficient way to keep cool. He fashioned a shiny black and white coat for me with special hair that deflects over 70 percent of the mid-afternoon heat!

My coat also provides excellent camouflage from my predators:

leopards, lions, cheetahs, hunting dogs, and spotted hyenas. When I stand behind a tree with jutting branches, my beautiful black and white stripes blend in with my surroundings. In the evenings when the light grows dim, other animals can't see me.

God thought of everything when he created me—**Mountain Zebra.**

Tell a Friend

The Mountain Zebra knows exactly where and how to stand in order to blend in with its surroundings. As Christians, we can do just the opposite. Instead of "standing in the shadows," we can ask God to give us opportunities to boldly share his love with others. We can make a difference in their lives.

Read About It

"Don't let anyone look down on you because you are young. Set an example for the believers in what you say and in how you live. Also set an example in how you love and in what you believe."—1 Timothy 4:12

Different types of zebras have different patterns of stripes. Researchers now believe that stripes are more than just camouflage. They help individual zebras to recognize other family members.

Pray About It

Lord, it's easy to blend in with the crowd, but I don't want to hide my faith! Thank you for helping me show your love through my words and actions.

When Temperatures Rise

My pot-bellied appearance makes me one of the chubbiest lizards around. Loose folds of skin hang around my neck and shoulders. I look like a smaller lizard trying to fit into its father's clothes!

Every morning I welcome the day by sunbathing on top of my favorite boulder. There I bask—all 16 inches of me—until my body temperature reaches a comfortable 100 to 105 degrees. That is when I begin my search for breakfast. I am 100 percent herbivorous, which means that I avoid meat. I hunt only for juicy desert plants—flowers, cactus fruit, leaves, and buds. God fashioned my body with special glands that help store water from the plants I eat. I also have a way to get rid of excess salt from the foods I eat: I sneeze!

God gave me a protective coat of armor, too—small scales all over my body. Larger scales guard my ear openings. Temperatures in the desert can change quickly from night to day. I can change, too. God taught me how to adjust my body colors from dark to light or from light to dark, to help control my body temperature. If it's a hot day, I'll turn a lighter shade to reflect the sun. When it's chilly, my color will darken to absorb more heat.

God thought of everything when he created me—**Chuckwalla.**

Tell a Friend

Have you ever heard an angry person described as someone who is "hot under the collar"? When the Chuckwalla's body temperature rises, it reflects the sun. Likewise, when we start to feel the heat of anger, we can turn to the Son—Jesus—for help. From the Bible passage below, we will learn how to control anger before it controls us.

Read About It

"Get rid of all hard feelings, anger and rage. Stop all fighting and lying. Put away every form of hatred. Be kind and tender to one another. Forgive each other, just as God forgave you because of what Christ has done."—Ephesians 4:31, 32

Lizards in Bible times scampered through king's palaces. Read about it in Proverbs 30:28.

Pray About It

I want to follow your example, Lord. When I start to feel "hot under the collar," help me to turn to you instead of lashing out.

Three Cheers for the Fishtronaut!

Have you taken a long walk lately? I wonder how many humans consider what it takes to walk, run, and jump without falling. Imagine what it would be like to lose your balance every time you tied your shoe or stepped out of a car. God knew the importance of balance and created your ears with a special fluid-filled canal. Tiny hairs sense every little movement. Each ear adjusts your balance according to the position you are in.

Well, guess what? Scientists discovered that my balancing system is much like a human's. They even decided to use me in a special experiment to prove their hunch. In 1998, one of my fish friends and I were plucked out of the waters near Woods Hole, Massachusetts. We became fishtronauts on the Space Shuttle Columbia!

Who would have thought a fish like me would ever fly three million miles into space? They wanted to see whether my pal and I would lose our sense of balance in a place without gravity. Would we be able to tell up from down, or would we get dizzy and topple over?

Being a famous fishtronaut was the high point of my life. You see, I have always been known as the ugliest, laziest fish around—a worthless creature in a big, cold sea. My Creator didn't see it that way, though. Out of all the fish in the sea, I was chosen for a special honor.

God thought of everything when he created me—**Oyster Toadfish.**

Tell a Friend

If a creature like the Oyster Toadfish has an important purpose in life, imagine how God can use each of us! Ask God to help you develop the abilities he has given you.

Read About It

"So God created the great creatures of the ocean. He created every living and moving thing that fills the waters. He created all kinds of them."—Genesis 1:21

My head is broad and flat, and some say I look like a gigantic tadpole, or baby frog.

Pray About It

Dear Lord, give me a heart of thankfulness so I can praise you for making me just the way I am.

The Snake That's Never Late

Snakes travel in different ways, just as people run, walk, skip, and jump. Some snakes crawl on the ground or side-wind on slippery surfaces where they can't get a good grip. Others swim, slither up trees, or burrow into holes in the ground. Not me! I am a flying snake!

I don't take off from a runway, and I don't depend on an air traffic controller to tell me where to fly. God gave me the ability to fly from one place to another, but I can't fly upward like an airplane or bird. I'm sometimes called a "parachuter," much like a flying squirrel. That means that I have to start my flight at a point that is higher than the place I want to land.

As I glide through the air, I hold my tail up higher than the rest of my body and wag from side to side for balance. The outer edges of my belly scales are rigid, while the middle scales fold upwards.

The angle of my scales acts like a parachute, slowing me down and prolonging my flight. I can travel over three times the length of a football field.

I live in the lowland tropical rain forests of southeast and south Asia. My home is in the trees there, so I am known as a tree snake.

I have an appetite for small prey like lizards, frogs, birds, and bats.

God thought of everything when he created me—**Flying Tree Snake.**

Tell a Friend

The Flying Tree Snake takes shortcuts by flying from tree to tree. We sometimes take shortcuts, too. When you are tempted to hurry through an important task, remember this: God honors those who work hard to complete a task to the best of their ability.

Read About It

"Work at everything you do with all your heart. Work as if you were working for the Lord, not for human masters."—Colossians 3:23

> I have ridges on my belly that help me grip smooth surfaces.

Pray About It

Thank you for giving me important jobs to do, Lord. Remind me to do my very best for you and to have a good attitude no matter what the task.

The Rain Forest Strangler

The rain forest is my home. I stand nearly 70 feet tall and measure 8 feet around my hollow trunk, but I wasn't always this size. Years ago, a bird deposited a seed from a fig it had eaten. The seed passed through the bird's digestive system and landed on a mossy branch. It quickly germinated and began sending out vines.

God provided lots of sunshine there at the top of my tall host tree. He protected me from fire and flood. Plant-eating animals could not nibble on my young roots up there, either. Year by year, my roots grew thicker and longer. They circled the tree like tangled limbs. I squeezed the tree trunk so tightly it quit growing!

As I grew, I sent out a thick umbrella of leaves to shade my host tree. It eventually died from lack of sunshine.

I used its hollow, lifeless trunk like an ivy growing on a lattice. God has given me a special job. I produce fruit year round, which provides nourishment for birds and mammals when other food is scarce.

I am an important part of the food chain in the rain forest.

As fruit-eating birds feast on my figs, the seeds pass through their digestive tract and are planted on other tree branches. New saplings start, and the process begins all over again.

God thought of everything when he created me—**Strangler Fig.**

Tell a Friend

The Strangler Fig has a purpose. It feeds animals at times when they might otherwise go hungry. God created you with a purpose, too—a perfect plan for your life!

Read About It

"God is working in you. He wants your plans and your acts to be in keeping with his good purpose."—Philippians 2:13

Pray About It

Thank you, Lord, for creating me with a special purpose in mind! Help me to understand it, so I can walk the path you have charted for my life.

Of the 800 or so fig species, about 200 of them wrap around a host tree and strangle it.

Giant Bell of the Sea

I'm a giant of the Arctic seas! I'm an *invertebrate*, which means I have no spine. I don't have a heart, brain, blood, or gills, either. I don't even have eyes, but I do have organs that sense light from darkness.

My body is called a bell because of its shape. It can reach a diameter of over 8 feet! On the surface of my bell is an opening like a mouth. Frilly arms hang around it, helping me capture and eat small animals called zooplankton. I'm able to smell and taste, even though I don't have a nose or tongue!

Longer arms, called tentacles, hang down in eight clusters. My tentacles are 98 feet long—longer than a blue whale! They are armed with stinging cells. Inside each cell is a special hair that sends a danger signal to me when it detects any movement nearby. Like a harpoon flying toward my victim, I can fire off a painful sting in just a few milliseconds—less than a second! My sting injects a poison that attacks the nerves of my victim.

I travel by riding the ocean currents and forcing water out of my bell to push myself around. God gave me a special way to stay upright: if my bell starts to tip, special nerves send a message to my muscles that tell them to tighten. That keeps me moving in the right direction.

God thought of everything when he created me—**Lion's Mane Jellyfish.**

Tell a Friend

A jellyfish probably won't ever sting you, but stinging insults are hurtful, too. Choose your words carefully, because once you say them, it's impossible to take them back!

Read About It

"Lord, may the words of my mouth and the thoughts of my heart be pleasing in your eyes. You are my Rock and my Redeemer."
—Psalm 19:14

I grow up to 8 feet wide, 100 feet long, and have up to 12,000 stinging tentacles!

Pray About It

Lord, help me to think before I speak and to choose words that bless, not hurt.

Keeping Cool in the Sonora

Who needs cool blue lakes with all this sand? Here in the Sonoran Desert, my friends and I keep cool by burrowing into a sand dune. The temperature 12 inches deep is often a whopping 50 degrees cooler than the surface sand. It's like changing from summer to winter in one quick leap. My snout works like a shovel, and I have a muscular neck, which helps me maneuver under the dune quickly.

God planned a way to protect my eyes and ears from all this sand. My eyes lock shut, thanks to tiny interlocking scales. Scaly ear flaps keep sand from filling up my ears, too. Nose valves save me from suffocation, and an upper lip overhangs like a miniature windshield.

I'm most famous for my unusual toes, which work like snowshoes. Covered with scales, they increase traction while I'm dashing across soft sand. If I can't outrun a predator, no problem; I just brake and burrow!

Temperatures in the desert can change drastically from sunrise to sunset. During milder temperatures, I stay above ground and blend in with my surroundings. My back is covered with bumpy, velvety scales that mimic the color and texture of sand. I have a built-in thermometer called a parietal eye. It's not a typical eye, but a sensor that alerts me when my body needs to cool down. When my temperature reaches a dangerous level, I dive under the sand and cool off quickly.

God thought of everything when he created me—**Sonoran Fringe-Toed Lizard.**

Tell a Friend

God taught the Sonoran Fringe-Toed Lizard how to escape from its enemies. In the Bible, God gives his people clear instructions on how to run from sin, too. It's the best handbook you'll ever own!

Read About It

"The name of the Lord is like a strong tower. Godly people run to it and are safe."—Proverbs 18:10

My family name is Phrynosomatidae. How's that for a mouthful?

Pray About It

Your way is always best, Lord. Help me to make good choices.

What a Laugh!

I hatched in a nest on top of a termite mound in the woodlands of eastern Australia. It was a safe place for a home because predators didn't bother the eggs there.

You might recognize my loud call. My hysterical "laughter" often echoes through theaters whenever a movie includes a jungle scene. It's how I announce my territory, and it gives my family a unique way to communicate with each other, too.

I never drink because my diet supplies all the moisture I need.

I spend most of my day poised on high branches overlooking the rain forest. My vision is sharp, and I can spot my next meal in a hurry. I swoop down and grab frogs, lizards, large insects, mice, and snakes up to three feet long.

I am not in a rush to leave the nest, but stay with my family for about four years. During that time, my parents assign me the duty of incubating eggs and supplying nesting material to keep the nest nice and cozy. You should hear us all laughing at once!

God thought of everything when he created me—**Laughing Kookaburra.**

Tell a Friend

The Kookaburra uses its voice as a tool to communicate. Its "laughter" travels through the jungle like a message on a loudspeaker. What does your voice—and the way you use it—say about you?

Read About It

"Thoughtless words cut like a sword. But the tongue of wise people brings healing."—Proverbs 12:18

Pray About It

Lord, I want my words to help, not hurt. Teach me to think before I speak, and to speak words that bless my friends and honor you.

Here in Australia, our loud call is known as a "bushman's clock." God gave me an unusual voice, and I use it at dawn, midday, and dusk.

Welcome to My Fruit Stand!

I'm famous along the slopes of the Andes because I am the only bear to live in South America. You could say I'm king of the hill! I tip the scales at 250 to 300 pounds, but am still smaller than most bears. I sport a shaggy reddish brown coat decorated by a cream-colored area around my mouth, throat, and chest. But my real claim to fame is the yellow rings circling my eyes.

God must have thought about how much time I would be spending up a tree. He custom-designed special claws for climbing. Sometimes I reach the top of a tree only to discover that the fruit isn't ripe yet. No problem! I just build a tree stand out of dry branches and wait. There I will stay for days at a time until the fruit is ripe enough to eat.

In addition to fruit, I like the taste of shrubs, honey, sugarcane, small birds, rodents, and insects. I've been spotted climbing a cactus to eat fresh spring flowers at the top, too.

My jaws are strong. They allow me the pleasure of tough treats like tree bark. I strip the bark off a tree the way you strip the peel off a banana (except you don't eat your banana peel).

I don't hibernate like other bears. That's because I can find plenty of food any season, so why sleep when there's a feast around every corner? Fortunately, I am not a picky eater. I eat foods that other animals refuse.

God thought of everything when he created me—**Spectacled Bear.**

Tell a Friend

The Spectacled Bear adapts well to change, season after season, and we can too. The Bible assures us that life's circumstances may change, but Jesus remains the same.

Read About It

"Jesus Christ is the same yesterday and today and forever."
—Hebrews 13:8

Read in 1 Samuel 17:33-37 how one Bible character wrestled with a bear and won.

Pray About It

Lord, it's nice to know that you never change! Thank you for helping me through times of change and for understanding how I feel.

97

Diving for Dinner

Before I hatched, my mother carried me in a bright orange egg sac. She sensed when it was time to build a nursery web around the egg case. She attached her bundle of eggs to a plant and wrapped an extra web around it for support. I stayed in the spiderling nursery until I was strong enough to begin life on my own. Then I headed for the water.

I now live on the steep bank of a creek in Ecuador. God taught me how to dash across the surface of the water without sinking. The tension of the water's surface prevents me from going under. He gave me hairs on the tips of my legs that help me tread water. I move so fast, I don't break the surface of the water. Unsuspecting tadpoles, insects, frogs, and fish do not realize I'm there. When I detect vibrations below, I dive into the water and wrestle with a wriggling victim. Then I carry it to a quiet place on the water's edge where I eat it all in one sitting. Imagine that! I measure less than an inch, yet I'm able to capture a meal many times my size.

I have an appetite that doesn't seem to end. In fact, a scientist recorded one of my cousins eating not one, but *two* tadpoles within 24 hours. That would be like eating several large pizzas all by yourself!

God thought of everything when he created me—**Fishing Spider.**

Tell a Friend

The Fishing Spider is small, yet mighty. No matter what age or size we are, God is able to use us exactly as we are. With God on our side, we can accomplish much! When we feel weak, we don't have to worry. God is a strong helper.

Read About It

"Look to the Lord and to his strength. Always look to him."
—Psalm 105:4

When I'm hungry, I brace my hind legs on a leaf or rock as I wait to spring into action. One silk strand anchors me to the shore, like a lifeline, just in case I fall.

Pray About It

Sometimes I feel too young or too small or too weak, Lord. Thanks for giving me your Word to remind me you are there to help me always.

I'm Not Crazy, Just a Little Cuckoo

People run from wasps, or swat at them, but my very life depends on them. I am a parasite—an insect that feeds off of other insects. I am also a wasp myself, which makes my life as a parasite a bit peculiar.

Some people call me a ruby wasp or jewel wasp because of my colors. I'm bright metallic blue, green, or red. You won't catch me standing still for long because I'm small, fast, and sneaky.

I hide near nests of wasps, bees, and certain other insects, such as sawflies and stick insects. I spy on them until the host leaves, then hurry inside and lay my eggs there.

Before I leave, I help myself to a snack of dead bugs—like a burglar raiding a refrigerator. Some of my favorite snacks are aphids, caterpillars, or spiders. There's a ready supply of them in a wasp nest since that is what wasps drag inside to feed their babies.

God gave me a strong covering, called a cuticle, in case an insect tries to attack me. It is thick, hard, and dotted with tiny pits. The underside of my abdomen is flexible, so I can easily roll up into a ball and play dead. I rarely sting, but if I am threatened, I have a small stinger that will stun an enemy.

God thought of everything when he created me—**Cuckoo Wasp.**

Tell a Friend

The Cuckoo Wasp is a parasite. All it does is take, take, take! God planned friendship to work the opposite. Give of yourself to a friendship, and it will bless you in countless ways!

Read About It

"A friend loves at all times. He is there to help when trouble comes." —Proverbs 17:17

Pray About It

Dear God, thank you for my friends. Show me ways I can bless their lives this week.

There are approximately 3,000 species of Cuckoo Wasps in the world, including about 230 in the United States and Canada.

A Furry Creature of Habit

If you were to spot me hopping through the snow, you might mistake me for a rabbit. But I'm much different from a common rabbit. Rabbits are born naked with closed eyes. I was born covered with fur with my eyes open. I could hop around almost from the time I was born.

I have unusually large, furry hind feet, which enable me to travel easily over snow. As I travel, I spread four long toes on each foot. That makes my feet even broader, like snowshoes. My Creator knew how easy it would be for predators to spot me moving along the white snow, so he planned a perfect way to protect me. In winter, my coat blends right in with the pure white of my surroundings. When warmer weather arrives, I begin shedding my fur, so that by summer my coat is a soft grayish brown. I blend in with every season!

I am a creature of habit. I travel back and forth between feeding and resting sites, using the same path every time. After several of my family members use it, the path looks like a snow-covered airport runway! By the time summer rolls around, we are so used to our route, we stick to it. If a plant blocks our trail, we just eat it!

God thought of everything when he created me—**Snowshoe Hare.**

Tell a Friend

The Snowshoe Hare sticks to the same path, no matter what the season. It is well traveled and takes him everywhere he needs to go. God promises to bless those who stay on track, according to his Word.

Read About It

"The path of those who do what is right is like the first gleam of dawn. It shines brighter and brighter until the full light of day." —Proverbs 4:18

Psalm 148 tells us that all of nature praises the Lord—even the snow beneath the feet of the Snowshoe Hare!

Pray About It

Lord, I want to be like the Snowshoe Hare, following the same path—your path—for all of my life.

Hippity-Hoppity Me

I'd invite you into my cozy, grass-lined home in Australia, but you're too big to squeeze down five feet of tunnels. I dug the burrow myself, according to God's blueprint. My sharp claws worked quickly, digging and smoothing our corridors. I'm at home here in Australia, but other members of my family live in meadows and at the edge of forests in the northern United States and Canada.

Please don't compare me to those drab gray field mice. *Harrumph!* I'm much prettier, if I do say so myself. My fur coat is two-toned: dark on top and yellowish-brown on my soft belly. A bold stripe runs along my sides where the two colors meet.

You won't find me snooping around your garage or running in the attic during cold winter months. I sleep nine months of every year. After my hibernation period, I awaken during the warmer months of summer.

Summertime is my busy season. I make up for nine months of inactivity by feasting on insects, leaves and stems, seeds, and berries.

At night, you'll find me hopping around my territory. That's right; I *hop!* God knew I'd need long, thin hind legs to spring me forward. He fashioned my tail extra-long to help me keep my balance. My body measures about four inches, but my tail is even longer. Altogether, I'm an eight-inch "mighty mouse."

God thought of everything when he created me—**Spinifex Hopping Mouse.**

Tell a Friend

God taught the Spinifex Hopping Mouse how to hop and where to find food at night. He teaches us, too, through his Word—the Bible. Share what the Bible means to you.

Read About It

"Trust in the Lord with all your heart. Do not depend on your own understanding. In all your ways remember him. Then he will make your paths smooth and straight."—Proverbs 3:5, 6

It's not unusual for me to share my burrow with other species of mice like me.

Pray About It

God, thank you for listening to my prayers and for keeping me on track.

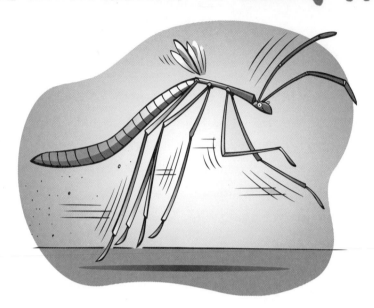

Stick 'em Up!

I began in an egg where I developed for 12 to 16 months. One warm spring night, I hatched in the cool, damp soil under a bushy clump of ferns. I pushed open my egg, quickly climbed a nearby stem, and rested and waited about 24 hours before I began my search for food.

I'm closely related to cockroaches, praying mantises, and grasshoppers. Females in my family grow wings, but are unable to fly. I am a male, and have the ability to fly if I need to. Because my wings are relatively small compared to my body size, scientists are stumped by how I can make it off the ground. I am over a foot long, but females of my species grow even longer!

In 1985, some of my cousins were chosen to travel on the D1 Spacelab mission, aboard a space shuttle! Experiments were carried out to study how low gravity and exposure to outer space would affect stick insect eggs.

Because I move so slowly, I'm not able to hurry down to a nearby stream when I'm thirsty. God knew I'd have a problem getting water when I needed it, so he made my body with special blood that helps me conserve water for long periods of time.

God thought of everything when he made me—**Giant African Stick Insect.**

Tell a Friend

God gave the Giant African Stick Insect a special way to deal with thirst. Did you know that people feel spiritually thirsty without God? We need him just as a thirsty person needs water. Long before Jesus came, Scripture predicted our Savior's arrival. Read how Jesus was described in the passage below.

Read About It

"He will be like a place to hide from storms. He'll be like streams of water flowing in the desert. He'll be like the shadow of a huge rock in a dry and thirsty land."—Isaiah 32:2

My wings are unusually small for the size of my body, but that doesn't stop me from flying. Scientists call me a "wonder of aerodynamics."

Pray About It

Dear God, thank you for sending Jesus to take away my spiritual thirst!

You Can Call Me "Sweetie"

Ilive underground in a fancy ant's nest—a maze of tunnels and domed chambers connected to one narrow vertical hallway. It doesn't look like a typical ant hill because it isn't a hill at all. Look closely, and you'll see ants coming and going through a narrow circular opening at ground level.

I'm a *replete*—a worker ant. Worker ants come in all sizes, and I belong to a group that is physically different from the others. God knew that I'd need a stretchy abdomen, called a crop. My crop serves as one of many storage tanks for the colony. During cool nights, I fill my crop with sweet nectar from flowers. Sometimes I add water, fats, and body fluid from insect prey, too.

Each colony has a unique odor. If I meet another ant during my nightly adventure, I quickly check to see if it is one of my nest-mates.

If a fellow ant from my colony needs a quick energy snack, we exchange honey mouth-to-mouth.

I live with other honey-gathering repletes in a special chamber at the bottom of the nest. Our room is a pantry for the colony—a well-stocked source of food. When my supply of nectar runs low, I go hunting again. During the rainy season, our community never suffers from a lack of food, thanks to my stretchy storage tank!

God thought of everything when he created me—**Honey Ant.**

Tell a Friend

The Honey Ant quickly recognizes members of its family. The Bible teaches us how believers in Jesus can recognize each other, too. When we are living for Christ, our lives reflect his love.

Read About It

"No one has ever seen God. But if we love one another, God lives in us. His love is made complete in us."—1 John 4:12

Pray About It

Dear God, I want others to see how much I love you. Help me to live my life so they will see Christ through me.

The ant is a hard-working creature. Read what the Bible has to say about the ant in Proverbs 6:6.

Today's Special: Savory Insect Stew

I'm a hardy plant that lives in the desert country of western Australia, where moisture is available to me only during the winter months. Rather than sentencing me to bake all summer long without water, God came up with an excellent solution. I live underground as a bulb during the hot months of the year. When cooler fall and winter months arrive, I poke my head up through the soil and drink in the rain like a thirsty pup.

Here in the dry desert, soil lacks the nutrients I need, so God planned another way for me to get the goodies I need to grow. He covered my round-tipped leaves with tiny droplets that look like dew. Insects climb onto my leaves for a drink of water, and a honey-like substance entraps them.

Slowly my leaves fold around their wriggling bodies like a blanket, soaking them in a digestive chemical. It's bug soup at its best! After my meal, I uncurl my leaves again to get rid of any leftover insect parts.

God thought of everything when he created me—**Sundew.**

Tell a Friend

The Sundew begins life with a single root. Without that taproot, it could not establish itself solidly in the ground and grow. As believers in Christ, we draw our nourishment from him. Read about how we can grow spiritual roots.

Read About It

"You received Christ Jesus as Lord. So keep on living in him. Have your roots in him. Build yourselves up in him. Grow strong in what you believe, just as you were taught. Be more thankful than ever before." —Colossians 2:6, 7

Pray About It

Everything I am and everything I have is because of you, Lord. Help me to depend on you and follow you faithfully all the days of my life.

As a young plant, I grew a taproot—a long root extending deep underground that delivered nutrients and moisture until I grew permanent roots that would support me for the rest of my life.

Vacuum Cleaner of the Sea

I might look like a vegetable that belongs in a tossed green salad, but look closer. I'm actually a soft-bodied relative to the starfish and sand dollar. I make my home in the Galapagos Islands. Marine biologists think I'm pretty special. In fact, they say I help turn over as much as 90 percent of the sea floor! My sifting work helps keep the seabed healthy, but I can live for five to ten years at any water depth.

My body is decorated with tiny tube feet. They work like mini suction cups, called tentacles, attaching me firmly in place. As I move from place to place along the ocean's bottom, my tentacles keep me rooted in place. Without them, I would drift aimlessly through the water.

God designed another group of tube feet near my mouth. These tubes act as my arms, although they're called feet. They're constantly in motion, sweeping the water around me like tiny vacuum cleaners. They bend and sway, capturing tiny bits of food, keeping me plump and pampered.

If a bully of the sea approaches, I play dead. It's the only way I know how to protect myself. I disconnect my organs quickly, including my two breathing tubes. Nobody messes with me if they think I'm already dead. Little do they know that I can grow a whole new set of necessary organs in just a few weeks!

God thought of everything when he created me—**Sea Cucumber.**

Tell a Friend

The Sea Cucumber's tentacles help "root" it, so it does not float aimlessly through the water. The Bible does the same for us, by giving us good advice to follow. Aren't you glad we can trust in God's care?

Read About It

"Let us hold firmly to the hope we claim to have. The One who promised is faithful."—Hebrews 10:23

In some parts of the world, I am considered a delicacy. Would you eat me for lunch?

Pray About It

Heavenly Father, I want to follow you. Help me to hide your Word in my heart.

Find Me If You Can!

When October storms chase away most bird species in Canada's alpine passes, you won't see me packing my bags. Nope! I am among a few hardy birds that stay put throughout the winter. A member of the grouse family, I am equipped to survive even the coldest conditions.

God created me with feathered feet that keep me warm and help me to waddle across snow without sinking. I have a chunky body with short legs, small wings, and a stubby tail. I spend most of my time on the ground like a chicken, so my feathered feet are perfect!

Like many of my cold-weather friends, I have a special camouflage that protects me from predators during snowy months. My feathers change colors three times a year. After wearing white feathers for winter, I change into a covering of gold, brown, and black.

By summer, most of my body has turned a chestnut brown. My change of "clothing" enables me to eat without fear of being attacked.

During winter, I feed by day, and by night I roost in snow burrows—tunnels dug into the snow. I spend the winter nibbling seeds and buds of trees like birch, willow, and alder.

God thought of everything when he created me—**Ptarmigan.**

Tell a Friend

God provides a protective covering for the Ptarmigan. Christians have a protective covering, too. Ours is not made of feathers, but is a strong head-to-toe armor! Read about it in the Bible passage below.

Read About It

"Put the belt of truth around your waist. Put the armor of godliness on your chest. Wear on your feet what will prepare you to tell the good news of peace. Also, pick up the shield of faith. With it you can put out all of the flaming arrows of the evil one. Put on the helmet of salvation. And take the sword of the Holy Spirit. The sword is God's word."—Ephesians 6:14-17

God gave me a keen sense for locating food, even when it's buried beneath snow.

Pray About It

Lord, you are my great protector. Thank you for equipping me from head to toe to live for you!

Can You Spell "Headache"?

I am the only wild white sheep in the world. God created me with a thick coat for warmth. Each hair of my coat is hollow, insulating my body while I explore the alpine ridges, meadows, and steep craggy cliffs of Alaska. Within hours of my birth, I was sure-footed enough to climb the steep slopes with my herd because the bottoms of my hooves are lined with a spongy, rough pad. They help me grip the ledges and cliffs where I run when I sense danger. I am light-footed and quick. From hoof to shoulder I measure about three feet, and weigh around 250 pounds.

Male members of my herd, called rams, butt heads in a fierce contest to see who is the strongest. We live together except during the mating season, so it is important for us to understand who is in charge. We are thickheaded, thanks to God, who created our skulls with a double layer of bone. That extra layer prevents injury during our head-butting contests.

It takes about eight years to grow a full set of horns. My horns are made of keratin—the same substance you have in your fingernails! Each year's growth produces a ring pattern on my horns, much like the rings on a tree. Count the rings, and you will be able to figure my age.

God thought of everything when he created me—**Dall Sheep.**

Tell a Friend

The Dall Sheep is sure-footed and strong. It faces its challenges head-on. When we face problems, the Bible has the answer we need. We can become as sure-footed as the Dall Sheep by following the example Jesus set for us.

Read About It

"He gives me new strength. He guides me in the right paths for the honor of his name."—Psalm 23:3

Jesus tells about the joy in finding a lost sheep. Read the story in Luke 15:3-7.

Pray About It

Father, I want to obey you. Help me stay sure-footed in your Word.

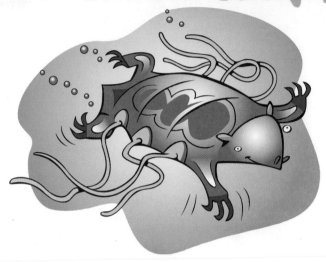

The Toughest Little Critter on Earth

My official name is *Tardigrade*—a big name for a tiny creature like myself. I'm both tiny and transparent, and measure about one-third of a millimeter long—about the size of the period at the end of this sentence. I'm a tiny freshwater animal with a short, plump body and four pairs of stumpy legs. Each leg has two-toed claws, which help me cling to plants. I dine on slimy algae and the plants upon which it lives. I lumber along like a miniature bear, stopping to picnic along the way.

You'll find me living in round, rain-soaked clumps of moss on shed roofs, gutters, or around ponds. Some of my relatives live at the base of trees, too. Don't expect to see me without the help of a microscope, though. Try soaking moss in water, then squeeze it dry. Drop some of the water on a glass slide and see how many of my family members you can find.

If my home freezes in winter or bakes in summer until it's dry, God taught me an emergency plan. I simply pull my legs in, shrivel up, and roll into a tight ball until things return to normal. If fact, scientists found one of my cousins that rolled itself up in a bottle of dried moss—for 120 years! When they added water, it perked right up.

God thought of everything when he created me—**Water Bear.**

Tell a Friend

The Water Bear has a God-given emergency plan for tough times. So do we! God does not to promise to spare us from problems, but he does promise to help us find a way through them.

Read About It

"The Lord saves those who do what is right. He is their place of safety when trouble comes."—Psalm 37:39

Pray About It

Dear God, help me not to shrink away when trouble comes, but to place my trust in you.

Scientists have tested my ability to survive tough conditions by exposing me to a temperature of 457 degrees below zero. I survived!

A Barking Duck on Stilts?

If you're ever trekking through the Andes Mountains of southern Ecuador, listen closely. Do you hear a barking sound? That's me calling!

Now, barking might not sound like such a big deal—except for one tiny detail: I happen to be a bird! I was discovered by an ornithologist (a person who studies birds) in the Andes Mountains of Ecuador in June 1998. He stopped in his tracks after hearing my strange bark. When I refused to come out into a clearing, he decided to trick me out of hiding. He tape recorded my barking voice, thinking that I would respond to another bird's call. Then he turned up the volume and waited.

Sure enough, I did think that another bird was calling. I hurried to within 25 feet of the tape recorder, where this enthusiastic bird lover could get a good look at me. Can you imagine the thrill of discovering a new species of bird?

I am a member of the antbird family—birds that follow army ants through the dense forest. Like a hungry traveler picking up leftover fruit in an orchard, I forage for insects left behind by armies of ants. God gave me springy legs that help me bounce from snack to snack like a pogo stick. Because I move quickly, ants don't have a chance to hop aboard my long, skinny legs.

God thought of everything when he created me—**Giant Antpitta.**

Tell a Friend

God gave the Giant Antpitta a unique way to communicate. Every person has a one-of-a-kind voice, too. What does your voice say about you? Are you patient and kind, or impatient and demanding?

Read About It

"There is a time to be silent. And there's a time to speak."
—Ecclesiastes 3:7

Of all the birds discovered in the past 50 years, I am the biggest. I guess that makes me a celebrity.

Pray About It

Help me think before I speak, dear God. I want to use my voice to bless others.

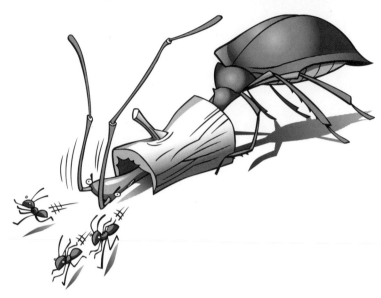

A Four-Inch Violin

If you were to visit the forests of Malaysia, you'd want to watch where you sit. You cannot just plop down on any old log or stump, because a sting from me could paralyze your fingers for 24 hours. God gave me a weapon to use in my defense—special glands that eject a fluid called butyric acid. He knew that I would need to be able to defend myself, even though I look creepy at four inches long.

I'm sometimes called a violin beetle because my shape resembles the stringed musical instrument by that name. My wing covers extend out in large, flat flaps at each side of my body. My whole body is flat, almost as if someone squeezed the air out of me. My flattened shape allows me to sneak into small spaces where I would not otherwise be able to crawl, like crevices, cracks in the soil, and under bark.

In the humid forests of Malaysia, I creep along in those tiny spaces in search of my next meal. Dinner usually consists of young insects. My head is longer than most beetles, which helps me to literally "stick my neck out" in my quest for food. It also helps me to peer into cracks and crevices before I enter.

God thought of everything when he created me—**Java Fiddle Beetle.**

Tell a Friend

God designed this beetle with a neck that helps it safely check out unknown territory before entering. In a similar way, the Bible tells us how to make wise decisions. God's Word will never steer us in the wrong direction!

Read About It

"God has breathed life into all of Scripture. It is useful for teaching us what is true. It is useful for correcting our mistakes. It is useful for making our lives whole again. It is useful for training us to do what is right."—2 Timothy 3:16

When my species was first discovered, insect collectors paid enormous prices for us. A good-looking beetle like me could sell for hundreds of dollars.

Pray About It

Dear Lord, your Word is like a long love letter to the world. Thank you for the way it helps me to know you better.

A Mean, Lean Fishing Machine

I'm not interested in munching my dinner from a little blue dish in the corner of a warm kitchen. No, thank you! I am a 29-pound cat who would rather leap into cold, swampy water than wait for a can opener. God created me to live wild and free.

A swampy region of Asia is my home. It's a perfect spot for satisfying a big appetite like mine. I fish the calmer rivers and streams here because I prefer fishing in the still waters of a marsh to swiftly moving currents. God gave me quick reactions, and it's a good thing! I have to know the exact second to leap into the water after my next meal, or I'll lose out.

I have special feet for swimming—four webbed feet with extra-long claws. My sharp claws are my fishhooks. I can either grab a passing fish with my fishhooks, or jump in headfirst and snatch it with my jaws, like a bear catching salmon. Once I land a slippery, wiggly fish, a claw makes an excellent dinner fork.

I am considered the best swimmer of all the cats in Asia. I'm not apt to curl up on anyone's lap for a neck scratching, though. I'm all business, and you won't ever catch me trying to purr my way into anybody's heart.

God thought of everything when he created me—**Fishing Cat.**

Tell a Friend

God equipped the Fishing Cat with everything it needs to care for itself. He taught it how to fish and survive in the swamps of Asia. What has God taught you to do well? How are you using your unique talents and abilities?

Read About It

"Work at everything you do with all your heart. Work as if you were working for the Lord."—Colossians 3:23

Pray About It

Lord, thank you for giving me special talents and abilities. Help me to use them wisely.

My double-layered fur coat keeps me warm even in cold water.

Mama Mia, It's a Mamba!

I began life in a warm, damp burrow in the ground. My mother laid over a dozen eggs there in my underground nest before deserting us. When the eggs hatched, we were already 16 to 24 inches long.

You'd better wear running shoes if you're going to travel with me. I travel 12 miles per hour—all 14 feet of me. I'm as long as an average male alligator! Members of my species live in pairs or small groups. I don't have to worry about predators because nobody wants to mess with me. Before antivenom medication was developed, my bites were always fatal.

I have a reputation as the most deadly snake in the world! My body is a brownish-gray color, and my back is brown and scaly. When I sense danger, I will raise my head and front body section four feet off the ground, open my mouth wide, and shake my head. I can strike from four to six feet away, and I'm usually accurate.

Once I strike a larger victim, I follow along while my poisonous venom works its way through the animal's bloodstream. When my victim becomes paralyzed, I prepare for a feast. God gave me flexible jaws that make it possible for me to eat an animal in one piece!

God thought of everything when he created me—**Black Mamba.**

Tell a Friend

At first glance, the Black Mamba does not look so deadly. In fact, it is a beautiful creature. Sin is like that; it wears a pretty disguise and tries to convince us that it can't hurt us. God will never trick us, though. He is always looking out for our good.

Read About It

"Watch and pray. Then you won't fall into sin when you are tempted. The spirit is willing. But the body is weak."—Matthew 26:41

When Jesus was preparing his 12 disciples to share the message of God's love, he advised them to be wise like a snake. See why in Matthew 10:16.

Pray About It

Dear Lord, give me strength and courage to make good choices. Help me turn away from anything that would pull me away from your path.

Eye to Eye

Y ou will not find me fluttering around the flowers in your backyard. My home is the deep tropical forest of Central America. Like many rain forest creatures, I am one of the larger members of my family.

Sometimes I am confused with the Owl Moth, but we're really quite different. Moths fly around only at night; while butterflies like me fly during daylight hours. My wings act as little solar heaters by continuing to warm my body long after I leave my sunny perch.

When resting, moths lie with their wings flat. Not me! I tuck my wings close to my sides, which exposes only my underside. I am easily identified by large *eye spots* on the bottom of my colorful wings. When I sense danger nearby, I flash my fake eyes. Those dark spots scare away intruders who mistakenly believe that they are the eyes of a wild beast.

My appetite for tropical fruit has earned me a bad reputation with local farmers. Back in my caterpillar days, a few hundred friends and I could damage an entire crop of bananas. However, my plain brown caterpillar days are long gone. You should see me now! I'm a brilliant powdery blue color with a wing span of around eight inches. I have relatives whose wings boast shades of gray, brown, orange, and purple. Together, we create a spectacular show around dusk when we feed off ripe bananas and other fruits of the tropical forest.

God thought of everything when he created me—**Great Owl Butterfly.**

Tell a Friend

The Great Owl Butterfly keeps others at a distance as a means of protecting itself, but God gives us human friends to share our lives. Have you told your friends how much they mean to you?

Read About It

"A friend loves at all times. He is there to help when trouble comes."
—Proverbs 17:17

My life span lasts from a few days to about eight months.

Pray About It

Thank you, God, for the wonderful gift of friendship. Show me ways to help my friend feel treasured.

Apartment for Rent

Everybody needs friends, and I am no exception. I'm a rain forest tree in South America, nicknamed an "ant tree" because the Azteca Ant uses me as an apartment building. My branches and trunk are hollow, and are divided into a series of chambers by partitions. My partitions are like hallways, connecting all the "apartments."

God created me with a special oil and sugary substance on tiny leaf hairs, and at the base of each leaf. My oil and sugar nourish a certain type of ant—the Azteca.

When Azteca Ants first arrive, the queen sets up a nest in a hollow chamber. Workers get busy in the other spare chambers until the entire tree becomes a colony of hard-working ants. The workers take what they need from me, but also protect me from insects and rain forest vines. The Strangler Fig, for example, would love to wrap its woody arms around my trunk and squeeze the life out of me. But it doesn't have a chance with Azteca Ants on board.

When my dangling fruit ripens, it attracts many different animals. Its seeds are a popular treat for birds, rodents, and other rain forest creatures. The animals digest the seeds, then replant them naturally when they leave piles of waste in the forest. The process starts all over again—just as my Creator planned.

God thought of everything when he created me—**Cecropia Tree.**

Tell a Friend

Have you ever heard the saying, "To gain a friend, you must be a friend"? The Cecropia Tree is a friend to Azteca Ants, and vice versa. They depend on each other for their very existence. Read below what the Bible says about the early church members and how they supported each other.

Read About It

"All the believers were together. They shared everything they had." —Acts 2:44

Azetca Ants benefit from a special partnership with the Cecropia Tree. Read in Proverbs 30:25 what the Bible says about the way ants diligently work to gather food.

Pray About It

Thank you for giving me such wonderful friends, Lord. Help me find ways to show them that I care.

Singing the Blues

Have you ever wanted to give your room a whole new look? Same here!

However, take it from me—a well-decorated living space does not happen overnight. It requires a lot of time, planning, and effort.

Here in the misty rain forest of New Guinea, I get my name from the thatched structure called a bower, which I build as part of my courtship ritual. A bower is not a nest, but a special place where I hope to meet a mate. I am a master architect, and my fancy bowers are so beautiful, bird lovers have photographed and studied them.

God gave me the instinct to fashion a U-shaped bower from strong twigs, leaves, and moss. Once the walls of my bower are set securely in place, the fun begins! I search high and low for blue objects to use as decorations in my new room. You won't find pinks or reds in my bower. I collect only blue feathers, flowers, berries, and shells, plus any shiny trinkets I can find. Before people arrived, I settled for blue items from nature. Now I'll take anything with a blue tint, from blue bottle caps and ink pens to clothing and paper.

While waiting to attract a mate, I stand guard over my fancy blue bower, so other young males don't steal my decorations. I also pass the time by painting my walls with a special mixture of crushed berries, saliva, and charcoal.

God thought of everything when he created me—**Satin Bowerbird.**

Tell a Friend

The Satin Bowerbird uses ordinary objects to create something beautiful. God can take an ordinary life, too, and turn it into something bright and beautiful. How is he decorating your life?

Read About It

"The same Lord is Lord of all. He richly blesses everyone who calls on him."—Romans 10:12

For nine months of every year, I am either building or remodeling my bower.

Pray About It

Lord, sometimes I feel very ordinary, but I know that to you I am EXTRAordinary! Thank you for loving and encouraging me.

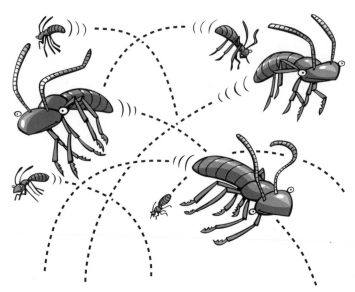

Flea on a Pogo Stick

If you live in a snowy part of the world, you might have noticed a sprinkling of black flecks across your front yard. It looks as if someone peppered the snow. Those flecks are actually my friends and me—tiny insects that come out on sunny days to chomp away at decaying leaf litter. We hop around and eat like we're at a potluck dinner, and some people confuse us for fleas. Our favorite foods are goodies like bacteria, fungi, and algae on the snow's surface. As snow melts at the base of trees, we lunch on leaf litter.

My official name is *Collembola,* but I'm sometimes referred to as a snow flea. I'm actually nothing like a flea, but you know how nicknames stick. God created me with two tails on my back end. Tucked underneath my belly, the tails are held strongly in place by tiny hooks. When I want to move, I unlatch my tails. They drop quickly, sending me shooting into the air. I look like a flea on an invisible pogo stick!

I don't feel the cold there on your snowy lawn because my black color absorbs sunshine. God takes good care of me while I work to help break down organic matter on the forest floor. You might call me a builder—a *soil* builder, that is. I digest plant litter, process it as waste, and return it to the soil.

God thought of everything when he created me—**Springtail.**

Tell a Friend

The Springtail serves an important purpose. It may be tiny, but it has a job to do! Its work makes a big difference in our world. Don't wait until you grow up to make a difference. Find someone who needs help and ask God to show you ways to help him or her.

Read About It

"We work together with God. You are like God's field. You are like his building."—1 Corinthians 3:9

Did you know the Bible mentions a flea in 1 Samuel 24:14?

Pray About It

Lord, I want to make a difference in my world. Help me to share your love with those who are in need.

Rhino with an Attitude

One-fifth of all the world's species are beetles, so I am in good company. I belong to the large family of scarab beetles. Some of my cousins live in North America, but are not as big as those of us who live in tropical forests. Although I'm harmless to humans, if you spotted my eight-inch frame lurking in the corner, you might run for cover!

My wings are encased in a tough, bony covering, like armor. If I were to get trapped underwater, I would survive by trapping air under my hard shell. God added breathing holes to my armor, too.

Sword-shaped horns curve over my head. We males use our horns in combat when we compete for a mate. We also fight for the best nesting site. I have a third horn, which sits in the middle of my head. It is shaped like the horn of a rhinoceros.

Each of my six legs sport a pair of claws called tarsi. They're so strong, I'm able to hang onto trees. Once I get a good grip, I'm nearly impossible to pry off.

God had a special reason for creating my family. Larvae provide a valuable food source for other animals. Adult beetles chew decomposing wood with our massive jaws. We help recycle material on the forest floor.

God thought of everything when he created me—**Rhinoceros Beetle.**

Tell a Friend

The Rhinoceros Beetle's armor comes in handy in difficult situations. Likewise, the Bible says that everyone who believes in Jesus has armor, too. Fully dressed in our spiritual armor, we can stand up courageously for our Savior.

Read About It

"So put on all of God's armor. Evil days will come. But you will be able to stand up to anything. And after you have done everything you can, you will still be standing."—Ephesians 6:13

When I fly, I make a whirring sound like a helicopter.

Pray About It

Dear God, thank you for protecting me with spiritual armor. Give me courage to live for you.

Life Inside a Chimney

On the ocean floor off the coast of Mexico, the earth's crust is cracking and shifting. I am a four-inch worm that lives inside a formation on the ocean floor known as a hydrothermal vent. The vents are scattered about like small doors in the sides of underwater volcanoes. A geyser of boiling toxic water shoots upward through the vents.

I make my home in papery tubes that I burrow into the sides of the chimneys. Hot water from inside the vent flushes through my chimney home and flows into much colder deep-sea water outside. God taught me how to position my head in the cool area and my tail where it's hot. Just imagine what it would be like to have the heat running in your living room, and the air conditioner blowing cold air in the room next to it!

Scientists are baffled by my ability to adjust back and forth between temperatures without turning into worm stew. They suspect that my hairy shawl—a fuzzy coat of hair hanging from my back like a fringed shawl—has something to do with it. They've gathered samples of my hair to study in special tests, and guess what? The hair contains proteins called eurythermal enzymes, which can stand all kinds of temperatures without being hurt! Scientists are hoping to learn more, and think that someday the proteins from my shawl will help them create new and better products, like medicines, paper, detergents, and textiles.

God thought of everything when he created me—**Pompeii Worm.**

Tell a Friend

Just as God prepared the Pompeii Worm to tolerate intense heat, so he can help you in times of trouble. If you've ever had a "heated" argument with a friend, you know how bad it made you feel afterwards. In the verse below, God has good advice for controlling hot tempers.

Read About It

"A gentle answer turns anger away. But mean words stir up anger."
—Proverbs 15:1

There are thousands of different species of worms in the world. The Bible mentions one type in Job 7:5.

Pray About It

Lord, I know that a hot-tempered argument can damage a good friendship. Help me to watch my words.

Riding the Waves

Imagine what it would be like to float across the ocean without a ship. I am a drift seed, and that is exactly what happened to me.

I grew in a paper-like seedpod on a long climbing vine called a liana. The vine hung from a tall canopy of trees in Central America. At the end of each vine bloomed a beautiful flower.

Inside the pod, I was covered with dense black hair. My fuzzy coating eventually wore off, exposing a tough, dark brown outer shell that looked and felt like wood. God made sure that it was waterproof, too.

My journey to the sea began when I fell from my seedpod to the forest floor. Heavy rains carried me to a river where I bobbed along for several days. I reached a sandy beach where the high tide finally swept me out to sea. There I joined thousands of drift seeds riding the waves. Some were shaped differently than me, but we all had one thing in common: God knew our final destination.

I ended up on a tropical beach, thousands of miles away from my rain forest home. If God had not planned ahead, I would have sunk to the bottom of the ocean. Inside my woody shell, he had placed a special air pocket. That little bit of air made me float!

God thought of everything when he created me—**Sea Bean.**

Tell a Friend

Just like a Sea Bean, God has equipped each of us for our journey through life. He planned every detail and knows our comings and our goings. He cares about what happens to us!

Read About It

"The Lord will watch over your life no matter where you go, both now and forever."—Psalm 121:8

Pray About It

Lord, you know me better than I know myself. Thank you for equipping me perfectly for the life you have given me.

Scientists studied one drift seed and determined that it had traveled 15,000 miles!

My Messy Claim to Fame

Mention the name pack rat, and eyebrows will rise. A pack rat is usually somebody who has a hard time parting with stuff. I earned the nickname because my most memorable trait is the way I build a midden and keep adding to it my entire life. A midden is an ever-growing heap of garbage and a "bathroom" area for critters like me.

Sometimes a midden is built apart from a nesting area, but occasionally members of my species feel so attached to their midden, they'll move into the heap and raise their babies there. That's exactly what I've chosen to do. To keep the pile from caving in on us, I glue my collection together with urine. The sun turns my urine into crystals, which holds the whole heap together. It's a way to mark my property, just as if I'd hung a sign that says, "Keep out!" on the doorway of my home. Scientists have found ancient middens still glued together after thousands of years, which allows them to study the living habits of my ancestors.

Besides my midden I build several food piles to last all through the winter. I don't hibernate, so my food needs are the same year round. And speaking of food needs—I am a favorite food of owls!

Researchers have decided that I stick close to home for fear of being hunted down and eaten. What do you think?

God thought of everything when he created me—**White-Throated Woodrat.**

Tell a Friend

A White-Throated Woodrat keeps everything. It builds its heap higher and higher as a way of saying, "This is my territory, so back off!" Do you surround yourself with material things instead of people? Are you missing some good friendships, or maybe special times with the Lord, because material things take up so much of your time?

Read About It

"You open your hand and satisfy the needs of every living creature."
—Psalm 145:16

When seeking food for babies, the females of my species wander as far away as 984 feet—more than three times the length of a football field.

Pray About It

Dear God, help me to enjoy the things I own, without letting them own me.

Get a Grip!

I'm rabbit-sized, and I wear a thick brownish coat that blends well
with the African savanna. I weigh about as much as a small sack of
potatoes and am 19 inches long. God knew that I would spend my life
climbing rocks, so on the padded sole of each foot he created a flap.
The flaps pull back, forming suctions cups! My front feet have four
toes and flat-bottomed nails that look like small bones.

My body does not adjust well to changes in temperature, so I
avoid grazing when it's too hot or too cold. My family and I sunbathe
by day and huddle together for warmth at night. All 25 of us squeeze
into our cozy rock crevice and pile atop one another like a stack of
hairy pancakes.

When we graze out on the open plains, we eat quickly to lessen
the chance that we'll be attacked. We communicate using various

sounds. When I was a newborn, I spoke with mews, like a lost kitten. Now I send messages by yelping, grunting, and when alarmed, squeaking loudly.

My upper teeth are triangle-shaped and look like little tusks. My lower teeth are like the teeth of a comb and come in handy for grooming. I am not a fussy eater, and I devour almost everything in sight, even plants that might be poisonous to other animals.

God thought of everything when he created me—**Rock Hyrax.**

Tell a Friend

The members of the Rock Hyrax family understand each other because they are good communicators. They say exactly what they mean and are good listeners, too. How well do you communicate with others when you are worried, happy, or afraid?

Read About It

"Turn all your worries over to him. He cares about you."—1 Peter 5:7

To avoid an attack while we're grazing, my family and I position ourselves in a fan pattern so we can keep a watchful eye out for party crashers.

Pray About It

Lord, I know I can tell you anything and you will listen. Thank you for hearing my prayers, even before I speak them.

Hairy Ol' What's-His-Name

I'm a critter with many nicknames. Some call me sun scorpion, even though I'm not a scorpion at all. Scorpions love sunshine, but I prefer to wander only at night. I am called wind scorpion because I look like I'm running as fast at the wind. Still others refer to me as sun spider because I make my home in sunny desert areas.

I belong to the family of arachnids—otherwise known as spiders. Worldwide, my family has 800 to 900 different species. In North America, there are almost 120 different types of arachnids. Imagine if we all showed up at your door!

If you run into me, it will most likely be at night—and I guarantee you won't forget me. God gave me four pairs of legs, but I use only three pairs to run. While scampering across the ground, I hold up my front legs and use them like a set of antennae. My bulky body is covered with hair, and my long legs span almost six inches! I am attracted to light, which is less than happy news to anyone reading by flashlight in a tent! Although I have a terrible reputation as a fierce biter, relax—I'm not poisonous.

Since I am not a hopping spider or a web-swinging spider, I rely on my speed and skill to hunt down and catch my prey. My favorite midnight snack is termites, but I'll settle for a nice juicy lizard, a grasshopper, or a crunchy beetle.

God thought of everything when he created me—**Camel Spider.**

Tell a Friend

The Camel Spider moves naturally toward light. So do people—except our light is Jesus. Read how his light changes lives for the better, both now and forever.

Read About It

"I have come into the world to be a light. No one who believes in me will stay in darkness."—John 12:46

God's Word speaks of a man named John the Baptist who wore camel-hair clothes and ate locusts and honey. Read about him in Matthew 3:1-6.

Pray About It

Heavenly Father, help me to share your light with my friends so that they can experience your great love.

I Smell Trouble

What is bigger than a robin, but smaller than a computer? Me! I'm a national symbol in New Zealand—a small flightless bird that locals refer to as their "honorary mammal." My family includes African ostriches, the rheas of South America, and the moa of New Zealand, which is now extinct.

I hardly resemble a bird at all. At the tip of my beak sit a pair of nostrils. I don't just peck at my food; I sniff it. I sniff and snort after spiders, earthworms, grubs, and fallen fruits before I eat them. I also use my beak to sniff out danger.

Tiny, two-inch wings look silly on such a plump, feathery body. I can't fly, but I *can* outrun a human. If a possum, pig, or ferret wanders near, watch out! My three-toed, clawed feet are weapons. I use them to kick and slash.

Like many birds, I mate for life. My mate cares for the nest and eggs, even to the point of not eating. Eggs take around 80 days to hatch, and a male can drop a third of his body weight during his time in the nest. God provides a special reserve of yolk in the belly of a new chick until it is three weeks old. It then leaves the nest with its father to search for food.

God thought of everything when he created me—**Kiwi Bird.**

Tell a Friend

The flightless Kiwi Bird does not sit around flapping its useless wings. It is too busy running, hunting, and caring for its family. God can turn our lives into something beautiful when we just ask.

Read About It

"We all have gifts. They differ in keeping with the grace that God has given each of us."—Romans 12:6

Pray About It

Help me to use the gifts you have given me, dear Lord. I want my life to make a difference in your world.

I lay one of the largest eggs of any bird my size. I am chicken-sized, but my eggs are as big as an ostrich's egg!

No Lily Pads for Me!

Move over, Spider-Man! I have extra-long toes, complete with toe pads to help me stick snugly to vertical surfaces. My huge webbed hands and feet make it possible for me to glide through the air like a bird. I simply spread my toes, take a leap—and I'm off! God designed my hind legs larger than the front because he knew I would need to push off when I leap from a branch. When spread fully, my webbed feet catch the air like a wind sail on a boat. I can glide easily for 50 feet.

My moist tropical home provides me with endless flights from tree to tree. I have a beautiful view from my treetop, too—a bright green rain forest canopy stretched out for as far as I can see. My back and legs glow a shiny green color in contrast to the undersides and in-between sections of my toes, which are a striking yellow. My body is only four inches long, but when I soar from tree to tree with my yellow sails, I measure one square foot!

Extra flaps of skin along both sides act as a built-in air control tool. As I near my target, special bones press firmly against my toes, readying my toe pads to grab onto the side of a tree trunk.

God thought of everything when he created me—**Wallace's Flying Frog.**

Tell a Friend

God thoughtfully prepared Wallace's Flying Frog with all it needs for flying. He cares for it from the time it pushes off a tree branch, to the moment its toe pads grab a tree trunk far below. God is busy preparing and equipping you for what he wants you to do with your life, too.

Read About It

"God's power has given us everything we need to lead a godly life."
—2 Peter 1:3

The Old Testament describes a time when frogs invaded the land of Egypt. Read about it in Exodus 8:1-15.

Pray About It

Dear Lord, help me to have the faith to turn loose of my doubts and fears and follow your perfect plan for my life.

Don't Expect Me to Quack!

When you're hungry, you head to the refrigerator, right? Not me; I dive deep and swim to the bottom of a river, where I feed at dawn and again at dusk. My warm, woolly undercoat and furry, waterproof outer layer are God's way of protecting my skin. The two layers work together to trap air to keep me warm and dry, even though I spend hours underwater.

My leathery, duck-like bill is perfect for stirring up mud in my search for shellfish, worms, and insects. Charged with tiny sensory nerve endings, it alerts me to predators nearby. My bill also helps me navigate around obstacles like rocks. I look like a duck, but don't expect me to quack!

I swim with webbed front feet and use my hind feet for steering and braking. God designed my hind feet to fold back against my tail when I'm not using them. A long, bristly tail helps me steer and keep my balance. If a human or animal tries to catch me, I zap them with a poisonous spur on my hind leg.

I don't hibernate like many animals. But during the colder months, I do take naps that can last up to six days! My body temperature falls in order to conserve energy, and I am inactive during that time.

God thought of everything when he created me—**Platypus.**

Tell a Friend

God keeps the Platypus warm, dry, well-fed, and protected. He provides everything we need, too. When's the last time you counted your blessings and named them one by one?

Read About It

"He has shown kindness by giving you rain from heaven. He gives you crops in their seasons. He provides you with plenty of food. He fills your hearts with joy."—Acts 14:17

When I dig my burrow, I fold back the skin of my webbed forefeet to expose claws.

Pray About It

Lord, you watch over me from morning to night, and even while I sleep. Thank you for blessing me so!

A Sweet Termite Trap

I'm a reddish-colored plant from the tropical forests of Borneo. God designed me with hollow-tubed growths at the end of my leaves, called pitchers. The upper edge of each pitcher is decorated with a white ring of tiny hairs, which provides sweet, nourishing nectar. One type of termite is drawn to the hairs and seems unable to resist. The rim of each pitcher is covered with slippery wax, and the pitcher itself is filled with digestive fluid. As they feed, termites slip down the opening of my pitchers and cannot get out. Then it's time for me to feed as I start to digest the termites—*yum!*

During one experiment, scientists placed Pitcher Plants across the path of some traveling termites. Sure enough, up to 22 termites per minute crawled up the plant, ate the hairs, and were soon trapped. Researchers peered inside and found thousands of termites from the same species trapped there. Once the hairs had been eaten, termites were no longer attracted to the plant.

Adult termites use my nectar for quick energy. Some manage to return home with nectar for their young, who need it to grow. I owe a lot to the tiny creatures that visit me—and to my Creator, who feeds me daily with a steady stream of termites.

God thought of everything when he created me—**Pitcher Plant.**

Tell a Friend

Termites are drawn to the Pitcher Plant by something that promises sweet refreshment. Sin is like that, too. It lures us to the "edge" with promises that it doesn't deliver. The good news is that we can resist temptation by turning to God for help.

Read About It

"You are tempted in the same way all other human beings are. God is faithful. He will not let you be tempted any more than you can take. But when you are tempted, God will give you a way out so that you can stand up under it."—1 Corinthians 10:13

God designed me to attract my prey with color, sugar, and smell.

Pray About It

Lord, it's great to know that I can call on you anytime and anywhere. Thank you for being my helper and friend.

A Fish Out of Water

I am a vertebrate—I have a backbone. I also have fins and breathe through gills. I am a fish, but also a member of the Goby family of amphibians. My home is located along a large bay near Japan. Members of my family live on tropical shorelines from Africa through Southeast Asia and the Philippines to Japan.

I'm a favorite subject of photographers who love to capture my flip-flopping, leaping courtship dance. If they persist, I'll run away by pushing myself along with my front fins. When I feel cornered, I'll dive into the mud. Photographers who don't give up their chase often end up knee-deep in the gooey mess. Now *that's* a picture!

How can a creature that breathes through its gills survive underneath all that ooze? God knows the secrets of my existence. He gave me an amazing collection of spongy sacs near my gills. As I breathe through my gills underwater, I absorb and store oxygen in my sacs. Like a diver with an oxygen tank, I can survive several minutes on land or buried in mud.

I need to roll in puddles often to keep my gills moist and free of mud. While bathing, I keep a close watch out for birds like herons, who consider me fast food. Most fish see clearly only underwater, but my bulging eyes see well on dry land for about 30 yards—almost a third of the length of a football field!

God thought of everything when he created me—**Mudskipper.**

Tell a Friend

God knows everything about the Mudskipper. He also knows all about you. He knew you long before you were born. God designed your exact eye color, hair color, and height long before you drew your first breath!

Read About It

"From the time I was born, you took good care of me. Ever since I came out of my mother's body, you have been my God."—Psalm 22:10

Pray About It

Lord, you have loved me forever. Help me to trust you more each day.

One of my mud-skipping relatives knows how to climb trees!

157

WHen Life Turns SHifty

I can hop faster than a person can run. A single leap will carry me more than six feet! Can you top that?

At first glance, people often compare me to a gerbil, but I belong to a different family that is known for its remarkable jumping ability.

My hind legs are four times longer than my front legs! I'm a silky, furry rodent with tan fur. My black tail tuft and facemask give me an air of mystery. If you picture me the size of a hopping kangaroo, think again. I'm only three inches long!

Members of my species live in desert regions of Africa and Asia. God knew I'd need extra help, so he designed my feet with tufts of bristly hairs under my toes and on the soles of my hind feet. The hairs help me to grip the loose sand. It's useful for kicking sand behind me when I dig a burrow, too. God designed my ears with a tuft of protective hair, which keeps sand from blowing into my ear canal. Wasn't that thoughtful of my Creator?

I may look cute, but I don't like to be handled. If disturbed, I growl, shriek, and thump my back feet. Otherwise, I'm a quiet loner.

God thought of everything when he created me—**Jerboa.**

Tell a Friend

The Jerboa gets a good grip on the loose desert sand, thanks to special footpads. God's Word helps us "get a grip" when we need extra encouragement in life. His promises never grow old!

Read About It

"Give praise to the Lord. Give praise to God our Savior. He carries our heavy loads day after day."—Psalm 68:19

Pray About It

Lord, thank you for loving me so much! When I need encouragement, you are always there.

In the late spring and summer, I plug my burrow to air-condition my underground home. It keeps the heat out and the moisture inside.

Quakin' in My Roots!

I began life as a single tree. Pioneer settlers to the United States nicknamed me "quakey" because my leaves would tremble at the slightest breeze. More recently, I have gained the nickname of *Pando*, which means, "I spread." Located south of the Wasatch Mountains in Utah, I am the biggest tree of my kind on record.

Passersby may think I'm just a normal grove of trees, but I am actually one 6,600-ton tree, spread across 200 acres! Biologists have studied tissue samples from all of the trees in my grove, and yep—I'm their mom!

Most trees reproduce by wind-blown seeds, but God planned another way for me to spread. New plants called suckers grew straight out of my roots. As the suckers grew upward toward the light, my strong roots provided nutrients and moisture, like a mother nursing a baby. Young trees supported by the roots of a parent tree have a better chance of survival than a single seedling. A tightly packed grove provides protection from too much sun, too. I have survived forest fires that burned neighboring forests to the ground because my roots will keep on producing new suckers.

My type of tree is the most widely spread tree species in North America. Our groves stretch the entire width of Canada, and scientists estimate that we cover tens of millions of acres in North America.

God thought of everything when he created me—**Giant Quaking Aspen.**

Tell a Friend

Do you "quake" at the slightest problem in your life? Remember this: When we invite Jesus into our hearts and lives, we are "rooted" in him. He will increase our faith as we depend on him day by day.

Read About It

"Have your roots in him. Build yourselves up in him. Grow strong in what you believe, just as you were taught. Be more thankful than ever before." —Colossians 2:7

Did you know the Bible compares kind words to a tree? Read about it in Proverbs 15:4.

Pray About It

Lord, thank you for helping me grow into the person you want me to be!

Take Two Mandibles and Call Me in the Morning

I belong to a group of hunter ants that move along the forest floor in a fan-shaped swarm. We attack scorpions, tarantulas, roaches, beetles, grasshoppers, and adult ants of other tribes. It does not take long for us to wipe out the food supplies of an entire forest area.

The queen of my colony can produce 100,000 to 300,000 eggs in a span of 10 days. When it's time for our colony to move again, we all work together like backpackers to help carry the babies, called larvae, to the new campsite.

We are helpful to people and to certain insects. Local people place one of us over a skin wound. The ant reacts by clamping down with its strong jaws, called mandibles, which naturally close the skin like a doctor's stitch. Then the person twists the head off the ant, leaving the mandibles clamped tightly across the wound!

Wasps, millipedes, and beetles often sneak into our ranks, spraying the pathway with a chemical that copies our scent. Our eyesight is so poor, we don't notice that they've joined our march. They benefit by eating meals that have been captured by our workers.

God though thought of everything when he created me—**South American Army Ant.**

Tell a Friend

It's easy to pretend to be someone we're not—just as the insects do when they mimic the army ants. God sees into our hearts, though. He knows who we really are inside because he has known us since before we were born. Are you allowing God to help you become the person he created you to be?

Read About It

"God, see what is in my heart. Know what is there. Put me to the test. Know what I'm thinking. See if there's anything in my life you don't like. Help me live in the way that is always right."—Psalm 139:23, 24

Proverbs 6:6-8 uses me as an example of hard work and cooperation.

Pray About It

Dear God, help me discover who I am and who I can become with your help.

Home Sweet Sock Drawer

During late fall, you might notice me hanging in a cluster on the side of your house or shed. My family and I are looking for openings around windows, doors, and foundations. Winter is coming, and we want in! Who needs scratchy bushes and trees when a warm, soft drawer full of socks is available? Who needs blustery winter winds, when there is a warm attic or wall to call home?

Once settled cozily inside, I'm not a demanding houseguest. In fact, I won't move or eat until late winter or early spring. You might not even notice me until my huge family and I start waking up in the spring. Then watch out! Our main goal is to find our way back outside.

Although I'm a harmless pest indoors, farmers and gardeners appreciate my help. God gave me a huge appetite for aphids—tiny insects that damage certain trees, roses, and crops. If the aphid population is too big for me to handle, I send out a special message by releasing a unique chemical scent. The scent attracts others in my family, and we plan a big aphid potluck.

God thought of everything when he created me—**Asian Lady Beetle.**

Tell a Friend

The Asian Lady Beetle looks for any opening in a house as a way to get in for the winter. Do you look for "openings"—opportunities—to be kind, to help others, or to share God's love? Be bold and persistent when it comes to doing good.

Read About It

"I will always guide you. I will satisfy your needs in a land that is baked by the sun. I will make you stronger. You will be like a garden that has plenty of water. You will be like a spring that never runs dry."
—Isaiah 58:11

I am the only lady beetle with a marking on my body that looks like the upside-down letter M.

Pray About It

Dear God, thank you for creating me with a special purpose in mind! Please guide me to the plan you have for my life.

Guess Who's Coming for Dinner

I live in the desert of the southwestern United States, where my enemies are few. I am an egg-bearing female wasp and must find a tarantula in which to lay a single egg. To me, a tarantula is like a snug, warm baby nursery. God gave me a keen sense of smell to locate the spider's burrow.

Entering the burrow is not as easy as you might think! Tarantulas line their homes with silk and stretch a silken trip wire outside the entrance as a gate. If an enemy wanders near, it jiggles the trip wire like a doorbell announcing a visitor. I love jiggling those trip wires because it lures the spider out of its shelter in a hurry.

I poke at the tarantula with my antennae until it rears up in a fighting position. We wrestle until I am able to maneuver in for a sting to its tender underside. I don't want to kill it because I need a live victim in order to carry out my plan. My poisonous sting paralyzes the hairy beast, but by the end of my attack, I am exhausted! I then probe the tarantula's open sting area and sip a "spider shake" from the fluid oozing there.

After that high-energy snack, I drag the hairy beast's body back inside its burrow where I lay a single egg on its back. My egg eventually hatches into a baby grub that feeds off the tarantula's body.

God thought of everything when he created me—**Tarantula Hawk.**

Tell a Friend

God gave the Tarantula Hawk a clear sense of how and where to lay its egg. If it ignores that plan, its efforts will not succeed. How well do you listen to God? When you sense that you are making a foolish decision, do you back off, or stubbornly proceed?

Read About It

"Increase my knowledge and give me good sense, because I believe in your commands."—Psalm 119:66

A tarantula has nothing to fear from males of my species, since they don't have stingers.

Pray About It

Forgive me for the times I stubbornly want my own way, Lord. Help me to listen instead of rushing ahead of you.

An Ant's Worst Nightmare

Move over, anteaters! I am a lizard with an appetite for ants, especially small black ants. Scientists estimate that I can eat anywhere from 600 to 3,000 ants in a single meal. I flick them one by one onto my sticky tongue.

When I am not gorging myself on ants, I work hard at keeping cool in my home in Australia's desert. I dig a shallow, underground burrow beneath small shrubs. I don't worry about predators, either, because God taught me how to protect myself perfectly: I change color to match the sandy soil. If an enemy finds my hiding place, I tuck my head between my front legs, leaving a knob-like bump that looks like a fake head.

Try to flip me over, and I'll press my spiny covering into the ground and refuse to budge. If that doesn't scare a predator, I can always puff myself up to appear larger. Are you scared yet?

God provides water exactly when I need it. My back is covered with thorns and tiny grooves in a pattern that resembles a system of canals. The grooves trap heavy dew or rain. When I need a drink of water, I gulp. That movement moves water along the grooves, to the corner of my mouth where I can drink as much as I need.

God thought of everything when he created me—**Thorny Devil.**

Tell a Friend

Think of a time when you were so thirsty, you could hardly wait to reach a water faucet. God promises us another kind of water—living water. Read the verse below and talk about what living water means to you.

Read About It

"Does anyone believe in me? Then, just as Scripture says, streams of living water will flow from inside him."—John 7:38

Pray About It

Heavenly Father, thank you for sending Jesus to quench my spiritual thirst!

I lay eggs in an air-filled chamber underground. When the eggs hatch, my young eat the shells as a valuable source of calcium.

169

A Hard Nut to Crack

Over 300 years ago, I was part of a lush tropical forest on Mauritius, an island in the Indian Ocean. I am a strong hardwood tree that island residents used as their main source of timber. In the early 1970s, a scientist noticed that I had grown old and sickly. He found only about a dozen trees of my species still alive on the island, each over 300 years old. Although we were still producing seeds, none of our seeds would sprout into new trees.

A hard-shelled outer casting protects my seeds. My seeds are so hard, they require a special process in order to sprout. They must pass through the digestive tract of an animal with a special stomach, called a gizzard, that grinds hard-to-digest food.

Centuries ago, the flightless dodo bird used to feast on my fruit. The seeds would pass through the dodo's digestive tract, and they ended up growing wherever he deposited a pile of waste. Over the years, hunters who visited my island killed so many dodo birds that they soon became extinct. Since no other animals ate my seeds, I was not able to produce new trees.

Scientists have been working hard to help my family of trees spread and grow again. They've discovered new ways to crack and grow my hard-shelled seeds with the help of wild turkeys. Someday the island of Mauritius may once again be full of my trees.

God thought of everything when he created me—**Calvaria Tree.**

Tell a Friend

God has equipped certain plants and animals for special tasks. Life goes smoothly for them when they work together. God also equips people to help and encourage others. Have you thought about how God could use your talents and abilities to help other people?

Read About It

"Teach me to do what you want, because you are my God. May your good Spirit lead me on a level path."—Psalm 143:10

God planned for certain plants and animals to help each other. Scientists call such partnership a symbiotic relationship.

Pray About It

My friends are a special part of my life, Lord. Help me to serve and encourage my friends when they are in need.

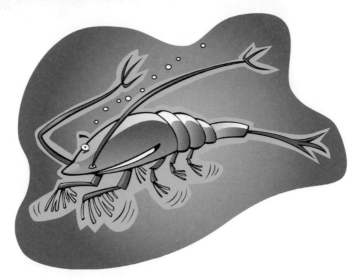

From Escape Artist to Parasite

I'm a small shrimp-like creature without a backbone called a crustacean. Some of my cousins live in lakes and ponds, but I live in the ocean.

God created me with many legs for swimming and gathering food. I feast on one-celled goodies like bacteria and diatoms. With a pumping motion, I suck the creatures toward my jaws, called mandibles, which process the food. And like a picky toddler, I sometimes spit out food I don't like.

Two sets of antennae keep me from sinking. They are also my built-in alarm system. Covered with tiny sensors, they let me know how fast the surrounding water is moving and alert me whenever there's sudden movement in the water. One simple eye in the middle of my head detects changes in light. God gave me lightning-fast reflexes that help me avoid danger. I'm a regular escape artist!

When I grow up, I will attach myself to a fish for life (I'm partial to Atlantic cod). I will no longer dart about, but draw nourishment from the flesh and blood of my host. As a female, I will spend the rest of my life producing eggs from my new home on the fin of a fish.

God thought of everything when he created me—**Copepod.**

Tell a Friend

Just like the Copepod, God wants to help us avoid harmful things. He wants us to seek his guidance when we're faced with big decisions or we're tempted by sin.

Read About It

"I will guide you and teach you the way you should go. I will give you good advice and watch over you."—Psalm 32:8

Pray About It

Lord, thank you for giving me guidance and wisdom. You take such good care of me! Remind me that you are just a prayer away.

Like a snake, I shed my skin 11 times during my development. At each shedding, I grow a little bigger.

My Glow-in-the-Dark Weapon

Life in the midwater ocean is cold and dark. Midwater is an area where sunlight cannot break through. At a depth of about 450 feet, light is either scattered or absorbed by the water. I live even deeper than that—about 1,300 to 3,500 feet below the ocean's surface. My brilliant red color appears black in the dim light of the midwater. God knew what he was doing when he painted me red. It's serves as a special camouflage!

Some of my shrimp cousins have been found living inside the shells of crabs, but not me. I like my freedom, so I swim in a large swarm. I look similar to a shrimp, except I have a deeper red color. I don't have to search very far for nourishment, because I like to feed on small particles of food that are left behind by fish that were too full to finish their meal. I'm about four inches long, but word has it that one of my relatives grew to be over a foot long! As an important member of the ocean world, I help process waste and provide food for young fish during the winter.

I am considered a delicacy by many fish and sea dragons. But guess what? God gave me a secret weapon to use when trouble comes near. If a predator starts to bother me, I spit out a special glow-in-the-dark fluid. My flashlight startles it and gives me time to escape!

God thought of everything when he created me—**Giant Red Mysid.**

Tell a Friend

God planned a way of escape for the Giant Red Mysid, and he will do the same for you. The mysid uses a special light as its secret weapon. God supplies believers with a powerful light through the Bible.

Read About It

"When your words are made clear, they bring light."—Psalm 119:130

More than 1,000 types of mysids live in the waters of the world. My species has an armored shell covered with spikes that discourage hungry predators.

Pray About It

Dear God, it is good to know that I can call on you in times of need. Thank you for always being there for me and lighting up my life with your love.

Scratching Out a Living

I was born in a gigantic nest called a mound. On the second day of life, I began foraging for food and drinking water all by myself. I did not have a mother or father to nudge me along. God taught me everything I know.

I am now a big-footed male bird with a mighty responsibility. To attract a mate, I must first prepare a mound, 15 feet across and 4 feet high. Using my claws, I rake leaves and other forest matter into a circle. From twilight to dawn, I work for days until my nest is finished.

Once satisfied, I hollow out holes where eggs will incubate. The nest must maintain a certain temperature or eggs will die, so God gave me a tongue that works like a thermometer! If I discover a cold section, I pile more leaves there—like adding another blanket to a bed. If I notice a hot spot, I open air holes.

After mating, a female lays one egg per hole, then runs away. That is when my real work begins! I monitor the nest's temperature for about two months. I also guard it from egg-loving predators like the Carpet Snake. Soon after hatching, baby Scrub Turkeys begin life on their own. My job is now complete—until it's time for me to build another nest, that is.

God thought of everything when he created me—**Australian Scrub Turkey.**

Tell a Friend

The Australian Scrub Turkey sticks to its job until it is completed. God gives us opportunities to show that we are responsible, too. In everything we do, we should work as if we are completing a job for him.

Read About It

"My dear brothers and sisters, stand firm. Don't let anything move you. Always give yourselves completely to the work of the Lord. Because you belong to the Lord, you know that your work is not worthless."—1 Corinthians 15:58

My hatchlings receive no parenting. Once they hatch, they are on their own.

Pray About It

Lord, help me to stick to the job you have given me to complete—even when it's tough or boring.

A Recipe for Trouble: Bounce, Shriek, and Run!

I'm a primate from the grasslands of Africa—a ground-dwelling monkey that avoids densely wooded areas. Scientists call me an omnivore because I eat whatever is available. I love to dine on pods, seeds, leaves, fruits, insects, eggs, lizards, and flowers of blooming trees.

Here in our family, called a troop, the highest-ranking female is in charge, while males guard our territory. As a male, I spend most of my time perched high in a tree or atop a cliff. I watch out for leopards, cheetahs, eagles, hyenas, and jackals. If a predator wanders too close, I start bouncing on a tree limb or bush. Making a lot of racket gives the rest of the troop time to sneak away or hide in the long grass. After the excitement dies down, we relax by leaning back and putting our feet up.

God colored my coat so that it perfectly blends in with the savanna grasses. It's mostly reddish brown, but the underside of my body is white or gray. I sport a long mane of hair around my neck and shoulders, and a white mustache.

God designed my body with long, slender arms and legs. If I'm threatened, I can run up to 35 miles per hour, which is the speed limit in most cities and towns!

God thought of everything when he created me—**Patas Monkey.**

Tell a Friend

The Patas Monkey knows what to do when it feels threatened: bounce, shriek, and run away. But we don't have to run away when problems come along. We can stand our ground and let God fight our battle for us.

Read About It

"When I am afraid, I will trust in you."—Psalm 56:3

> We're usually quiet, but our troop will bark when meeting another troop along a path.

Pray About It

Lord, it's nice to know that I don't have to run away from problems. Thank you for being my protector, my helper, and my Savior.

Knock Knock!
Anyone Out There?

I develop inside a warm, cozy egg for about two months. My shell was not very big, and there came a time when I needed fresh air. God planned a way for me to break out of my hard shell. He created a special tool that I could use for slicing through the soft inner layer. However, that's not all; he knew I'd need something extra hard to crack open the rock-hard outer layer of shell, too.

His solution was an egg tooth—a tough chunk of skin that sits on top of my snout. Formed long before I was ready to leave the security of my egg, the egg tooth was ready before I needed it. When the big moment arrived, I used it as my ticket to freedom.

First, I rubbed the tip of my snout up and down inside the egg. Then I whacked the shell a few times to split open the hard outer layer. I used my egg tooth only once. After bursting out of my shell into the fresh air, I no longer had a use for it. Several weeks after I hatched, it disappeared back into my body, never to be seen again. It had served its purpose by doing the important job God planned for it to do.

God thought of everything when he created me—**Crocodile.**

Tell a Friend

Our Creator oversees the birth of a Crocodile by giving it a way to crack its own egg. The Bible tells us that God watches a human baby as he or she develops, too. He orchestrates every detail of those early months and longs for us to trust him for the rest of our lives.

Read About It

"None of my bones was hidden from you when you made me inside my mother's body."—Psalm 139:15

Pray About It

Thank you for the gift of life, dear God. Help me to use it in a way that brings honor to you.

Certain adult saltwater Crocodiles have been known to swim for over 600 miles between islands or around coastlines.

Mighty Mouth
of Madagascar

Mention my name and people shudder. Nobody likes me. That's because I remind them of a certain insect that is viewed as a filthy pest. You see, I am a member of the cockroach family. But not all roaches are created equal, and I don't look or behave like that dirty roach that scampers for cover near a garbage can.

I live on the damp forest floor in Madagascar, an island off the southeast coast of Africa. Since I am a cold-blooded insect, my body temperature adjusts itself to the temperature of my surroundings. I'm four inches long, and I weigh almost as much as two sticks of butter!

I am definitely not an ordinary roach. For one thing, I don't stink, and neither do my droppings. I don't have wings or wing pads. I'm chocolate brown with dark orange marks on my abdomen. During the day, I hide under debris while I wait for nightfall. If I'm bothered,

I'll let loose with a hiss that is meant to scare off intruders. My signal alerts the other members of my colony who quickly join in. Sometimes we hiss just for the sake of hissing, like a choir warming up for its opening song.

God thought of everything when he created me—**Madagascar Hissing Cockroach.**

Tell a Friend

The Hissing Cockroach's body adjusts to the temperature of its surroundings. When the temperature is hot, it heats up. When a cold wind blows, its body cools down. Make sure that outside influences—like certain friendships—don't dampen your relationship with God. Stand up for what you believe, no matter what other people think.

Read About It

"Lord, may the words of my mouth and the thoughts of my heart be pleasing in your eyes. You are my Rock and my Redeemer."
—Psalm 19:14

Some people keep me as an exotic pet. I thrive on dog biscuits, lettuce, and celery.

Pray About It

Dear God, I want to walk close to you, no matter what everyone else does.

My Life's a Masquerade Party

Certain entomologists (people who study insects) think I'm related to the lowly cockroach. *Harrumph!* If you ask me, my species is much more creative than a cockroach. We are masters of disguise. Some of my relatives have fancy bodies like flowers. They look so convincing, insects land on them in search of sweet nectar! Others have the God-given ability to change their coloring to blend in with their surroundings.

I look like a crinkly, brown leaf. Most people and predators pass right by without realizing I am an insect. I use my disguise as a protection against my enemies, as well as a way to sneak up on my next meal.

I have over 2,000 cousins. I've heard rumors that some of my family members are kept as pets, but in Malaysia, we can grow six to ten inches long! Would you want an insect that size lumbering around your bedroom?

God designed my body with an extra-long neck. It enables me to move my head back and forth 180 degrees. I have two large eyes on the sides of my triangle-shaped head for viewing images and color. Three smaller eyes between my antennae help me detect darkness and light.

When hungry, I react quickly. My claw-like legs dart out, hook an unsuspecting cricket or lizard, and CRUNCH—he's history! If I'm extra hungry, I can grab and hold one critter while munching on another. You could say I'm an excellent multitasker.

God thought of everything when he created me—**Dead-Leaf Mantid.**

Tell a Friend

The Dead-Leaf Mantid is a master of disguise. Sometimes people try to disguise their true feelings from others, but nobody can fool God. He invites us to relax and just be ourselves.

Read About It

"But God is greater than our hearts. He knows everything."
—1 John 3:20

My eyes are sensitive to the slightest movement up to 60 feet away!

Pray About It

Lord, thank you for loving me the way I am. Help me to love myself as you do, so I can be the person you created me to be.

Orange-Eyed Night Stalker

I'm a giant among my species and the largest owl in Europe, with a wingspan of six feet! Females weigh almost nine pounds. My scientific name is *Bubo bubo*. How would you like to go through life with a name like that?

God specially designed my feathers to be speckled with brown and black. He knew that I'd need plenty of camouflage during the day so I could rest without being bothered by predators. I sleep by day and hunt all night.

My ears are located on the side of my face. One of my ears sits a little higher than the other one so I can locate the exact direction of a sound! God molded a feather pattern around my eyes to form a dish shape. It works like a funnel, carrying sound into my ears. My eyes are a beautiful shade of orange, and I have perfect vision. With eyes and ears working together, I'm sure to have a good night's hunt.

My partner and I met during a mating season, then built a nest together. We will stay together for life. Favorite nest sites for birds of my type include a cliff, rock crevice, or behind a bush on the ground. Some of us choose a nest that another large bird has abandoned.

God thought of everything when he created me—**Eagle Owl.**

Tell a Friend

The Eagle Owl has an unusual scientific name—*Bubo bubo.* How do you feel about your name? Did you know that when somebody asks Jesus into their heart and life, he gives them a brand new name? Wearing the name "Christian" is a giant responsibility because others will judge Jesus by the way we live and act.

Read About It

"Dear children, don't just talk about love. Put your love into action. Then it will truly be love."—1 John 3:18

The male Eagle Owl prepares several nest sites, then advertises them by clucking loudly. The female then tours each site and selects one as their home.

Pray About It

Lord, I want to make a difference in this world. Show me everyday ways I can share your love with others and bring honor to your name.

Saltshaker of the Shoreline

I was planted on the Mediterranean shoreline as a windbreaker—a tree that slows the force of strong winds blowing in off the sea. I am able to tolerate the harsh, dry climate and salty soil of this region. If I were to catch fire or were chopped down, I would send up new shoots and start again.

Tourists sometime wonder if I have died because my small, feathery leaves give me a wilted appearance. But inside my bushy branches is a survivor. I can live in soil that has hardly any nutrients. I don't require fresh water, and there on the shores of Crete, I soak up to 1,100 liters of salt water every day. Talk about thirsty!

God showed me how to expel excess salt from seawater. It collects on the tips of my leaves like powder and discourages insects from munching on me. Thanks to salt, I am free of parasites and disease.

I grow a foot per month every spring and will produce up to 500,000 windblown seeds. New trees have sprung up all around the world. Some were even discovered growing high in the nearby mountains at an elevation of 7,000 feet!

God thought of everything when he created me—**Tamarisk Tree.**

Tell a Friend

Strong winds and a blazing sun cannot destroy the Tamarisk Tree. In much the same way, God helps us to stand against problems that blow into our life. With his help, we can weather anything.

Read About It

"But I will bless any man who trusts in me. I will show my favor to the one who depends on me. He will be like a tree that is planted near the water. It sends out its roots beside a stream. It is not afraid when heat comes. Its leaves are always green. It does not worry when there is no rain. It always bears fruit."—Jeremiah 17:7, 8

The Bible says that Abraham planted one of my ancestors in Beersheba. Read about it in Genesis 21:33.

Pray About It

Lord, help me to understand your Word, so that I can stand strong when problems blow into my life.

Welcome to the Hotel Amazonica

I'm an extraordinary plant with floating leaves that measure up to seven feet across—more than the height of an average man! I'm at home in the warm waters of South American lakes and rivers.

God created a partnership between a certain Amazon beetle and me. The beetle is attracted to my bright white flowers, which measure a full foot across and smell like a butterscotch and pineapple dessert. The blossoms open wide at night to provide a cozy 98-degree room for my insect friend. Inside my petal hotel, this large brown beetle feasts on sugars and starches.

The petals close as the flower cools, tucking the hungry beetle in for a cozy sleepover. God arranged for my flower to release pollen at dusk. When my flower opens up the next morning to release the beetle, it flies away with its body covered with pollen. As the beetle searches for a new food supply, my pollen drops onto other flowers.

Once a flower has been pollinated, it sinks underwater and forms a seed-filled pod. The new seeds eventually float to the surface, where water carries them along to a spot where they will begin a new plant. Then the cycle will begin all over again, just as God planned.

God thought of everything when he created me—**Victoria Amazonica.**

Tell a Friend

God schedules meetings between beetles and the Victoria Amazonica, and he plans special meetings in our lives, too. Think of friends he has brought across your path. Ask God how you can touch their lives with his love.

Read About It

"Lord I will praise you among the nations. I will sing about you among the people of the earth. Great is your love. It is higher than the heavens. Your truth reaches to the skies."—Psalm 108:3, 4

Named in honor of Queen Victoria of England in 1838, Victoria Amazonica is the largest water lily in the world.

Pray About It

Thank you for the friends you have given me, Lord. Help my friendships to grow and show me ways to share your love with others.

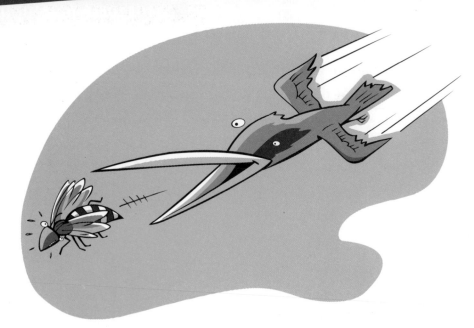

Bring on the Bees!

I roost in a small colony of brightly colored birds like myself. We live high in the treetops along coastal areas of Africa, the Middle East, and from Russia to Asia. I'm a stunning shade of green with—you guessed it—blue cheeks!

Don't expect to find me pecking for worms like a robin on a damp lawn. I thrive on a steady diet of stinging insects like hornets, wasps, ants, and bees! Other birds would not dare try to catch a bee, but what's the big deal?

I perch on a high wire or tree branch until I spot my prey. If a bee lands near me on a branch, I ignore it. God gave me instructions to catch insects only during flight. Catching them off guard is the key to a successful hunt. I swoop down and snap up my clueless victims before they know what hit them.

God custom-designed my bill for chasing down bees. My long, narrow bill is positioned a safe distance from my eyes, so an angry bee can't deliver a blinding sting. Once I catch a bee, I whack it several times against a tree branch, or give it a big strong squeeze to rid it of venom. Then it's lunchtime.

God thought of everything when he created me—**Blue Cheeked Bee-Eater.**

Tell a Friend

God has taught bee-eating birds how to avoid a painful and poisonous sting. Did you know words can sting, too? When someone says something hurtful, how do you react?

Read About It

"Lord may the words of my mouth and the thoughts of my heart be pleasing in your eyes. You are my Rock and my Redeemer.
—Psalm 19:14

Because I thrive in sunny climates, you won't find me anywhere in Britain.

Pray About It

Lord, I can't control how others treat me, but I can control my reaction to their words. Help me to turn to you instead of trying to get even.

Anteater of the Air

I live in Indonesia, where I feed on ants and termites. I am an eight-inch lizard that is often compared to a hang glider. While some people occasionally hang glide for fun, it's how I travel every day! God outfitted me with over a dozen ribs connected by flat folds of skin.

When I spread my "wings" and push off from a branch high above the forest, I sail majestically through the air for more than 150 feet—three times the width of a basketball court!

I'm a beautiful sight as I soar across the rain forest—a mixture of green, blue, and yellow orange. If I fold my wings tightly against my sides, I blend in perfectly with my surroundings. I rarely touch the ground because the ants that I eat live in the trees with me. When I'm hungry, I hang on the side of a tree trunk, waiting for ants to come close enough to grab without moving. Researchers have called me a "sit-and-wait feeder."

Every day between 11 AM and 1 PM I take a break from my normal gliding and feeding activities. By doing so, I avoid the hottest hours of the day. I never glide when it's windy or raining, either. If a predator is hot on my trail, I automatically start climbing the nearest tree.

God thought of everything when he created me—**Flying Dragon Lizard.**

Tell a Friend

Think of a time when you wished you could just soar above your problems, rather than solving them. Did you ask God for help? If not, why not?

Read About It

"Think about the ravens. They don't plant or gather crops. They don't have any storerooms at all. But God feeds them. You are worth much more than birds! Can you add even one hour to your life by worrying?"—Luke 12:24, 25

The Bible says that when we trust in God, he will give us strength when we're weary and help us to soar like eagles. See Isaiah 40:31.

Pray About It

Lord, you help me to rise above my problems. Thank you for teaching me to let go and trust you completely.

Pink Parents of the Lagoon

I'm four feet tall, but only weigh 16 pounds. That's less than some Thanksgiving turkeys! My long skinny legs are perfect for sifting through mud in the soggy coastal lagoons of South America. God gave me an oversized, curved bill, but no teeth. I have a large tongue, which forces water and mud through a sort of filter. The filter collects food like worms, insect larvae, and tiny plants like algae and diatoms.

My webbed feet have four toes—three in front and the fourth high at the back. These feet would not work for an animal that needs to climb, but my Creator knew I would need to steady myself in the slippery lagoon. My feet grip mud like suction cups.

For the sake of safety, my mate and I live in a colony of several thousand birds. The two of us built a nest out of mud and vegetation. Our nest is six to twelve inches high, with a twelve-inch hollow area in the top. When I breed in the spring, I lay a single oblong-shaped egg in that spot.

Both of us take turns sitting on the egg for 28 to 31 days each.

After welcoming our grayish white chick into the world, we take turns feeding it, too. Our baby will not be able to fend for itself until it is about two months old, but together we prepare it for independence.

God thought of everything when he created me—**Flamingo.**

Tell a Friend

God equipped the Flamingo with feet that would help steady it from falling. The Bible also keeps us from falling by increasing our faith and strengthening our commitment to Jesus.

Read About It

"The Lord is faithful and will keep all of his promises. He is loving toward everything he has made."—Psalm 145:13

Pray About It

Thank you for being a trustworthy Savior and Lord. Help me to know you better through your Word.

Some of the food in my diet contains high amounts of a special pigment called carotene. If I eat a lot of it, it will turn my new feathers pink and red.

Hoses and Gaskets and Wiring, Oh My!

I live in the alpine region of New Zealand, where my family of parrots has a reputation for being extremely curious. We are unafraid of people and new environments. In the mid-1800s, our curiosity got us into big trouble. We were attacking sheep with our sharp curved beaks, which caused bacteria to enter their bloodstream through their wounds. Farmers hired hunters to kill us, and close to 150,000 parrots were shot. Today, our population only amounts to a few thousand parrots.

God created me in shades of green, blue, yellow, and red. I have a curved bill that acts like a set of portable tongs, making it easy for me to collect seeds, rootlets, insects, and larvae. I attract crowds and have been called "the clown of New Zealand's southern Alps." But tourists don't think I'm so funny when they discover that I have eaten the rubber strips in their windshield wipers!

There's no end to my pranks. I like to roll stones down the iron roofs of mountain huts and steal the contents of backpacks. I can shred hiking boots in a short time and love stealing sunglasses.

I'll never win a popularity contest, but I'm still considered one of the world's most intelligent, beautiful, and curious birds.

God thought of everything when he created me—**Kea.**

Tell a Friend

Sin can be a heavy burden until we face it and ask God for forgiveness. Don't be like the Kea, who "plays dead" when he's caught. Admit your sin, turn away from wrong behavior, and ask for God's forgiveness.

Read About It

"Then I admitted my sin to you. I didn't cover up the wrong I had done. I said, 'I will admit my lawless acts to the Lord.' And you forgave the guilt of my sin."—Psalm 32:5

Members of my parrot family have been known to steal keys and then play dead when their deed is discovered.

Pray About It

Heavenly Father, thank you for lifting the guilt of my sin. Teach me good judgment, so I can make choices that honor you.

Tic-Tac-Toe . . .
Watch My Web Grow!

At first glance, my web looks like a normal spider web, but step closer. See those thick zigzag lines in the shape of a large X? Researchers have tested them and discovered that they are made from a different kind of silk than I use for the rest of my web. Those strands reflect ultraviolet light, which trick flying insects into thinking my web is a fancy flower.

I cling to the zigzag X and wait there with my eight legs separated in pairs. From a distance, I look like a dangling game of tic-tac-toe. My feet have three claws each—one more than most spiders.

When an insect flies into my web, I wrap its body in strands of silk until it can no longer move. Then I ring a dinner bell. *Yummy!*

If a hungry predator tries to catch me, I have an emergency plan. God created me to vibrate my web so the outline of my body is blurred. If that does not confuse my visitor, I can flip through an escape hatch to the other side of the web, then drop to the ground. I can also wiggle my abdomen to expose a pair of large black dots—scary, fake eyes. That usually does the trick!

God thought of everything when he created me—**St. Andrew's Cross Spider.**

Tell a Friend

God created the spider to know a way of escape. It instinctively knows how to run from danger. Jesus provides a way of escape for us, too. With his help we can run from temptation.

Read About It

"When you are tempted, God will give you a way out so that you can stand up under it."—1 Corinthians 10:13

Pray About It

Lord, when I run into a sticky web of temptation, help me to remember that it's never too late to turn away. Thank you for giving me an escape hatch where I can seek help from you.

The Bible teaches that anyone who forgets God is like a person who leans on a spider's web. Find out more by reading Job 8:13-15.

Mini-Hippo, Pig, or Deer?

My strange appearance would give a dentist nightmares! God gave me special teeth called tusks that actually look more like antlers. Instead of growing out of my mouth, my canine teeth grow through the upper part of my snout. They curve upward and back against my head. Although they look threatening, they're actually rather brittle and can break easily.

My family lives in small groups in the rain forest. Most of us are around three to four feet long, with a foot-long tail. I tip the scale at 200 pounds. I have a pudgy body, bristly skin, long snout, and small ears. My long, skinny legs speed me along to my favorite wallowing hole where I spend hours trying to rid my skin of parasites.

Mothers in my family build a soft, grassy nest for their babies. They give birth to only one or two babies at a time. Our lifestyle provides plenty of playmates for the young of our family and helps us band together to watch out for predators. Trails connect our territory, almost like sidewalks connecting a neighborhood. We visit each other often, like friendly neighbors or cousins.

By day, we are excellent runners and swimmers, which has helped our species establish new colonies from island to island along the coast of southeast Asia. At night, my family and I graze on grasses and feed on fruits, bugs, leaves, and water plants.

God thought of everything when he created me—**Babirusa.**

Tell a Friend

The Babirusa appears to be a pig, yet has the characteristics that make animal experts wonder about its identity. Christians take on a new identity when they ask Jesus into their hearts. When we allow his love to shine through us, others will notice a difference.

Read About It

"Anyone who believes in Christ is a new creation. The old is gone! The new has come!"—2 Corinthians 5:17

I communicate with a low grunt or a moan. When I'm excited, I clatter my teeth.

Pray About It

Lord, help me to live for you so others will notice my true identity as a follower of Jesus.

I Get Carried Away

I was named for J.F. Wolff, an 18th century German physician and botanist (a person who studies plants). I am the world's smallest flowering plant and a member of the duckweed family.

God created me without roots, so I don't require soil. I simply float on the surface of a body of water, such as a pond or a quiet stream. Part of me is visible from above as a delicate flower, and the rest lives underwater. If you were to rub me between your fingers or hands, I would feel like fine grain or meal. That is why I am sometimes referred to as "watermeal." I look like fine green grains floating in the water.

When my fruit bursts, my seed sinks to the bottom of the pond, but that's not the end. God planned an awesome voyage for my tiny blossom. Water birds, such as ducks, land in the pond, and seeds stick to their feet. Because birds tuck their feet close to their bodies in flight, it's easy for seeds to hitch a ride from pond to pond! In the southeastern United States there are records of plants being carried by a tornado, or frozen inside hailstones!

God thought of everything when he created me—**Wolffia.**

Tell a Friend

Even the tiniest flowering plant in the world can spread and grow, thanks to God's plan. As believers in Christ, we play an important role in spreading his love. Are you treating others in a way that helps them to see Jesus' love?

Read About It

"Dear children, don't just talk about love. Put your love into action. Then it will truly be love."—1 John 3:18

Pray About It

Lord, thank you for loving me so much. I want others to know your love, too. Help me to pass your love on to my friends and family who don't know you.

I measure less than 1/25 of an inch! My fruit is smaller than a grain of table salt! It is even smaller than a single cell of many plants and animals.

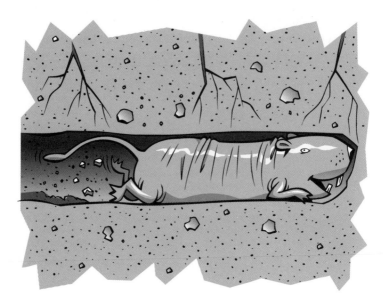

A Naked Tunnel Digger

I'm a small rodent with hair so fine and pale, it barely shows. Two teeth hang out of my mouth like mini tusks. I've been nicknamed a "hotdog with teeth."

Here in the hot, dry region of Africa, our family structure is often compared to that of ants and other insects. We have a queen, soldiers, and workers, and each group is responsible for certain tasks. We work hard, cooperating with each other to get the job done. Cooperation makes life run smoothly down in our burrow home.

God knew all along that I would be a tunnel-digger. He prepared me for that job by giving me a strong jaw muscle. It is considered the strongest jaw of any mammal my size. God also knew that I would need a way to keep dirt out of my mouth while digging. He attached extra folds of skin to both sides of my mouth to carry dirt away from my face like a drainpipe.

My home is an underground freeway system with tunnels that lead to various rooms. It has a feeding room where we share our roots and tubers and a nesting area where we sleep. We all lie in a big heap for warmth.

We can't smell anything, so if a newcomer from another colony enters our home, we accept him as one of our own. As far as we are concerned, if he looks like us, we must be related. We welcome him and put him to work.

God thought of everything when he created me—**Naked Mole Rat.**

Tell a Friend

Each member of the Naked Mole Rat's colony does its job without grumbling. So should we! If you rake yards, rake to the best of your ability. If you wash dishes, find a way to make it fun. When everyone pulls together and does a good job, a home runs smoothly.

Read About It

"All hard work pays off. But if all you do is talk, you will be poor."
—Proverbs 14:23

I live in a colony of 20 to 300 individuals. Our family structure and work habits are similar to that of bees, wasps, ants, and termites.

Pray About It

Dear God, thank you for giving me work to do and for equipping me to do my best.

A Deadly Surprise

I grew from a long strand of about 30,000 eggs, laid in a small pond by my mother. A male toad fertilized the eggs, and within three days we had hatched. I looked like a typical jet-black tadpole—tiny, wiggly, and cute. My shape changed quickly, though, and I turned into a toadlet and hopped away one day.

I'm now a hefty, warty amphibian from Australia—a toad that looks and behaves much differently from other toads. You'll recognize me by the bony ridge above each eye and the oversized glands on both my shoulders. God planned those glands so I would have a way to protect myself. They produce poison, called venom, which I am able to ooze if an enemy bothers me. I have smaller poison storage glands spread over my entire warty body.

When a predator comes too close, I flip over on my side and point my shoulder glands at it. An animal receiving a dose of my poison will die within 15 minutes! If a sneaky intruder tries to eat me, he'll be in for a deadly surprise, too. I'm a poisonous snack even as a tiny toadlet. Humans can't escape my wrath, either. Those who try to trap me quickly discover that my venom can cause intense pain and temporary blindness.

God thought of everything when he created me—**Cane Toad.**

Tell a Friend

God provides animals like the Cane Toad with a way to protect themselves from predators who would harm them. God gives believers his Word as a strong shield. Which verses have helped you in times of trouble?

Read About It

"God's way is perfect. The word of the Lord doesn't have any flaws. He is like a shield to all who go to him for safety."—Psalm 18:30

A few native animals of Australia have learned how to snack on only my nontoxic parts.

Pray About It

Thank you for sending your Word to protect me. Teach me to depend on it daily.

Hold the Mayo, I'm Not a Tomato!

On the east coast of Africa lies a place called Madagascar. It was there on the surface of a swamp, my mother laid over 1,000 tiny eggs. Within two days, I hatched as a tadpole. Then about 45 days later, I changed into the cutest little froglet Mom had ever seen.

I am now the color of a vine-ripened tomato. It took several months for me to reach this brilliant orange red color. Every now and then, if the humidity and temperature is not to my liking, my pretty coloration changes to a drab brown.

Males of my species grow to be two and a half inches long, but we females are larger. I measure almost four inches long and have a hearty appetite. I am what scientists call an "ambush hunter." At night, I sit and wait until my prey comes along, then I spring forward to catch my dinner. I will eat just about anything that moves, including files, moths, crickets, mealworms, worms, and grasshoppers.

God designed my head with a special muscle in my skull. When I shut my eyes, the muscle pulls them downward into my head cavity. I also have a unique mouth. Instead of teeth, God formed the roof of my mouth with rows of ridges, which help smash and grind my meals.

Got thought of everything when he created me—**Tomato Frog.**

Tell a Friend

The Tomato Frog changes during bad weather. Sometimes our friends change when life gets difficult. Some people only want to be your friend when times are good. These people are known as "fair-weather friends." Aren't you glad God is not like that?

Read About It

"I give you a new command. Love one another. You must love one another, just as I have loved you."—John 13:34

Pray About It

Lord, thank you for sticking with me during the good times and the bad times. Help me to be a faithful friend to others no matter what they are going through.

If the temperature turns unseasonably warm or cold, I have a simple solution— I hibernate.

Flashlight of the Amazon

I'm a rare insect with a lot of nicknames. My family originated in China, but I live near the Amazon River in South America. I was born with a long forehead and a large, snout-like growth on my head. Curving upward, my snout's bumpy design looks like a peanut shell. My odd-shaped head is hollow and leads down into my digestive tract. The main attraction—every now and then my head lights up like a flashlight!

Some people in this region are afraid of my light. They believe that a bite from me means sure death. That's not true, though, because I don't bite! I have a special mouthpiece like a drinking straw, which I use to suck nutrients from plants.

God gave me a creative way to protect myself: I pretend I'm a lizard, like the lizards that scurry along the branches of my favorite feeding trees. I also try to scare intruders by opening my wings and flashing two bright red and black spots at them. The spots look like huge eyes. If that doesn't work, I give up and spray them with a chemical. My body manufactures the spray as the result of eating toxic tree resins. The resin doesn't make me sick, but the resulting toxic spray will stop an enemy dead in its tracks.

God thought of everything when he created me—**Lanternfly.**

Tell a Friend

The Lanternfly uses caution when meeting other creatures of the rain forest. It imitates a lizard! The Bible tells us we should imitate Jesus. He loves us and will never lead us in a wrong direction.

Read About It

"You are the children that God dearly loves. So be just like him. Lead a life of love, just as Christ did."—Ephesians 5:1, 2

Pray About It

Thank you for setting an example that I can follow, Lord. Give me courage to stand up for what I believe.

People of the Amazon rain forest also call me "alligator bug."

A Gentle Aussie Giant

I glide gracefully through the water off Australia, thanks to my skirt-like fins. They're thin and hang in billowing folds along my sides. When I squirt a jet of water out of special funnels, watch out! The water hits those fins and propels me forward. By pumping water in and out of my gas-filled cuttlebone, I am able to control how deep or shallow I glide through the water.

I'm the biggest type of cuttlefish, reaching a length of over three feet. Two gigantic eyes stare out at my world from my broad, flat head. Ten tentacles extend from my head also, waving like arms in an underwater ballet. Two are feeding tentacles, which can be reeled in when I'm done foraging. How's that for a portable fishing pole?

God taught me how to protect myself against predators. He gave me the ability to change the color and texture of my skin to imitate rocks, sand, or plants. Or I can sink to the bottom and rapidly pump water out of my funnels to bury myself in the sand.

If all else fails, I'll shoot a blob of an inky substance as a decoy, or create a cloud of ink in hope of escaping behind it.

God thought of everything when he created me—**Giant Australian Cuttlefish.**

Tell a Friend

Actors memorize lines and try to imitate the character they are portraying—like the Cuttlefish imitates rocks, sand, and plants. But God doesn't want you to pretend with him, since he already knows everything about you. You should always be honest with God.

Read About It

"God is spirit. His worshipers must worship him in spirit and in truth."—John 4:24

Underneath my fins and tentacles is a spongy, chalk-like shell called a cuttlebone. It gives shape to my body like a skeleton.

Pray About It

Lord, you know me better than anyone does. I'm glad I can relax and just be myself with you.

A Blossoming Friendship

The yucca is an amazing flowering plant, divided into about 40 different types. It is known for the amazing way it pollinates. *Ta-da!* That's where I come in. I'm a moth with the God-given ability to stuff a tiny ball of pollen into the cup-shaped center of each flower. The yucca plant needs me so much, if I don't show up it stops producing seeds. Imagine that—a plant who waits for a certain moth to arrive for duty!

Moths like me can be found in the southwestern United States and Mexico, plus certain areas of the Caribbean Islands. Each spring, male and female members of my species slither out of our cocoons and fly to nearby yucca plants.

I lay my eggs in a yucca flower and deposit a rolled ball of pollen into the stigma of the plant. As pollen grains germinate, they send hundreds of fertilized seeds deep into the flower's ovary. When my larva hatches during late spring and early summer, it awakes in a "room" surrounded by flowers and delicious food.

By early autumn, the larva emerges from its feeding room and drops to the ground. There it burrows into the rain-softened soil and builds a silky cocoon. It stays inside its cocoon during the long rainy months of winter. When the temperatures finally warm up, an adult moth emerges and begins its search for—what else?—a flowering yucca plant.

God thought of everything when he created me—**Yucca Moth.**

Tell a Friend

The yucca plant and moth have a partnership that works perfectly. A good friendship follows that same pattern of give and take. How do you and your best friend give to one another?

Read About It

"Love each other deeply. Honor others more than yourselves."
—Romans 12:10

The Bible compares an evil person's house to a moth's cocoon. Read about it in Job 27:18.

Pray About It

Thanks for being a good friend, Lord, and for setting an example for me to follow.

Too Hot to Handle

Stand back, you ant! I have a boiling-hot surprise for you—a stinky toxic spray that I can aim perfectly, no matter where you try to bite me.

German scientists discovered that my body manufactures two special chemicals. Alone, the chemicals are not harmful—but combine them and *KABOOM!* An explosion takes place that results in the trigger-fast release of my chemical spray.

Each chemical is stored in a separate chamber along with a third chemical, called an inhibitor, which prevents them from exploding too soon. A tightly fitted ring of muscle separates the chambers. I relax the muscle when an enemy approaches, which allows the chemicals to flow together. Like a skilled chef, I add one final ingredient—a fourth chemical—which sends a message that it's time for an explosion.

Researchers from Cornell University used a special camera to record how fast I could respond to a predator. They poked and prodded me with a small pair of forceps to imitate an ant attack. Each poke brought a perfectly aimed spray to the forceps.

No matter where the researchers poked me, I knew how to swivel my abdomen and discharge the spray to the exact spot. My amazing weapon never missed its mark.

God thought of everything when he created me—**Bombardier Beetle.**

Tell a Friend

The Bombardier Beetle has a weapon that guarantees victory over ant attacks. The beetle's weapon is fast and always accurate. The Word of God is described as a spiritual weapon. It protects us from spiritual attacks that try to destroy our trust in the Lord.

Read About It

"The word of God is living and active. It is sharper than any sword that has two edges."—Hebrews 4:12

I carry enough chemicals at any given time to fire off 20 to 30 shots, one right after the other.

Pray About It

Thank you, God, for providing the Bible as a strong weapon for those of us who have placed our trust in you.

Partners for Life

If you searched all day, you still wouldn't find me. I am a bacterium that's visible only through the lens of a microscope. Some bacteria are harmful, but God gave me a specific job to do. I carry out my duties by living in soil and inside plants.

First, I attach myself to the root hairs of a plant. That's when the fun begins! Once I set up housekeeping, I release a substance that causes them to curl. A team of us forms a line and spreads deep inside those roots. Like an army, we split into groups and go to work. We invade bumpy growths on the plant's stem called nodules.

I am considered nitrogen-fixing bacteria because green plants need me. They are unable to use natural nitrogen directly from the air, but thanks to God, I know the formula for changing natural nitrogen into a simpler substance called nitrate. Green plants need nitrates to live. See why I love my job?

I help the plant, and the plant, in turn, helps me. Cells within those bumpy nodules supply oxygen for me to breathe. The plant also provides a safe home and steady supply of carbon, which gives me energy. The carbon is produced from light—sunshine! My army of bacteria and I work together in a friendly partnership to help our host plant grow tall and strong.

God thought of everything when he created me—**Rizobium.**

Tell a Friend

God created microscopic bacteria and plants to work together as partners, and he created men, women, boys, and girls to live in harmony, too. Are you helping or hurting your friendships?

Read About It

"A friend loves at all times. He is there to help when trouble comes."
—Proverbs 17:17

Pray About It

Please forgive me for the times when I act uncooperative, Lord. Show me how to give of myself, as Jesus did.

> Cows can thank me for the nitrogen in the grass they eat.

Life Inside the Slime

I hail from the coast of Ireland, where I live inside a thick, slimy tube buried on a beach. I am found in a sheltered harbor or other areas that don't have a lot of foot traffic. You might also find me tucked under tiny rock ledges near starfish or anemones in a tide pool.

I grow to about eight inches long and one inch wide. If a predator bothers me, I can pull back inside my protective tube. I do this by shortening the length of my body to half its normal size, similar to the way a turtle behaves when it retreats into its shell. God taught me to filter water through my gills in order to catch anything worth eating. I'll dine on plankton or other small food that happens to float by me.

A giant nerve fiber stretches the entire length of my body. It is one of the largest nerve fibers in the animal kingdom. Because this nerve is so big, scientists are happy to study as many of us worms as possible. By inserting special probes into our bodies, they can test how fast our nerves are able to conduct electricity.

God thought of everything when he created me—**Slime Worm.**

Tell a Friend

When trouble shows up, the Slime Worm does a disappearing act. What about you? How do you handle discouraging times? God has good advice for both good times and not-so-good times—keep trusting in him!

Read About It

"The Lord is good. When people are in trouble, they can go to him for safety. He takes good care of those who trust in him."—Nahum 1:7

Pray About It

Dear God, you are worthy of my trust. Thank you for hearing and answering my prayers.

In Psalm 22:6-8, King David cries out to God in his time of need. He says that his people are treating him poorly "like a worm."

Something's Fishy

My mother laid her eggs in a jelly-like substance. Her eggs floated on the surface of the sea in sheets until they were ready to hatch. I hatched as a female. I am a most unusual fish, with a special growth hanging from my forehead. It lights up to guide me through the murky waters along the sea bottom, where I forage for food. When it's time to mate, the soft glow of my light also attracts a male of my species.

After mating, we stick together for life—literally. The male grips my skin with sharp, pincer-like teeth *(ouch!),* and from that day on, I tow him through the water like a trailer. To attract my next meal, I wiggle the "flashlight" lure on my forehead.

Over the next few weeks, strange things happen to my mate's body. His skin becomes spiny and fuses with mine at his jaw area. His eyes grow smaller and finally dissolve. Only two holes remain open, one on each side of his mouth. Those allow him to draw in water for breathing.

It's a good thing God gave me a stretchy stomach so I could eat for two. My mate eventually receives food directly from my bloodstream, which now begins circulating through his body, too. Now, how weird is *that?*

God thought of everything when he created me—**Anglerfish.**

Tell a Friend

God takes delight in his creation. He didn't bring us into the world and then forget about us, but lovingly provided a guidebook—his Word—as a "flashlight" to light our way! How well do you know your Bible? Memorize a verse every week with a friend, and by the end of one year, you'll each know 52 new Bible verses to light your way.

Read About It

"Your word is like a lamp that shows me the way. It is like a light that guides me."—Psalm 119:105

The Bible contains a lot of very fishy stories! Read Matthew 14:14-20 to see how Jesus used two small fish.

Pray About It

Thanks, Lord, for giving me your special guidebook, the Bible, to show me how to live.

Stare Down with a Gecko

A couple of years ago, my mother laid two eggs on the African island of Mauritius. The eggs were connected, and she held them pressed tightly together with her hind legs until their shells hardened. Then she abandoned them. Two or three months later, my brother and I entered the world as hatchlings.

Life is one journey after another, but I am well-equipped. My toes are padded with bristly, microscopic hairs. At the end of each bristle, God installed between 100 and 1,000 tiny suction cups which allow me to walk up walls and cross ceilings upside-down.

I am one of the world's smallest reptiles. My scaly covering is designed in a pattern of striking colors like blue, red, orange, gold, and green. I look more like an ornate beaded purse than a reptile.

If you and I were to have a staring contest, I would win. My oversized eyes don't have lids, so I never blink! Fortunately, God gave me a long, sticky tongue that keeps my eyes moist and clean.

During the day, I forage for food while I hop along tree branches. At night, I find a smooth branch where I can sleep. I know a lot of predators would love a tender "geckowich" for dinner. But if an enemy grabs me, my tail breaks off, and I scamper away. I don't worry because another tail will grow back in a few days!

God thought of everything when he created me—**Ornate Day Gecko.**

Tell a Friend

When someone hurts or annoys us, wouldn't it be nice to be able to leave the "broken" part behind, like the gecko? Life doesn't work that way, but the Bible does give us guidelines for handling sticky situations. Read about it below.

Read About It

"You have heard that it was said, 'Love your neighbor. Hate your enemy.' But here is what I tell you. Love your enemies. Pray for those who hurt you."—Matthew 5:43, 44

Day Geckos like me benefit humans by helping to control the insect population.

Pray About It

Thank you for sending Jesus as an example of true love. Help me to love and forgive others just as Jesus does.

A Prickly Hitchhiker

I ride from place to place by hooking onto socks, shoes, or other clothing. If livestock or a pet brushes against me, I'll cling so tightly, it takes scissors to remove me. My burs contain air spaces that allow me to float for up to 30 days, too, so if I fall into a stream it's not a problem.

I grow on a plant in the middle of a wet, weedy field. My plant needs 15 full hours of darkness. Darkness helps release a protein pigment that tells me when to produce flowers! A single burst of light is enough to stop this process, so my plant never blooms during summer.

I may be a lowly weed, but God used my sticky burs to spark a good idea. In 1948, a Swiss mountaineer, George de Mestral, went on a nature walk with his dog. When they returned home, Mestral's dog was covered with burs. Mestral was curious and inspected the burs under a microscope to see how they managed to cling so tightly to his clothes and to his dog's fur.

He noticed a hook-and-loop design, which led him to create a two-sided fastener that we know as Velcro®. Velcro is used in backpacks, shoes, and by NASA, to keep equipment from floating around in the weightless environment of space.

God thought of everything when he created me—**Cocklebur.**

Tell a Friend

God uses even those sticky, hitchhiking Cockleburs. Have you considered how he can use your talents and abilities, too? Why not ask him where he'd like you to begin?

Read About It

"God's gifts of grace come in many forms. Each of you has received a gift in order to serve others. You should use it faithfully."—1 Peter 4:10

The seeds of my pods were eaten either raw or cooked by Native Americans. The cooked paste was applied to puncture wounds.

Pray About It

Heavenly Father, sometime I feel as useless as a wild weed. Please show me ways I can make a difference in my world.

Neighborhood Snoop

What bird drops walnuts onto a busy highway so cars can run over the nuts and crack their shells? It's me—a bird that is considered crafty, intelligent, and an extreme pest.

Nothing escapes my notice. I perch at the top of trees to spy on other birds that are building nests. My brain records the location of each nest. I also watch birds carrying food back and forth to their babies. Many a nest has been robbed of its tasty young because of my sharp memory.

My feathers are a purplish-black color, but my bill, legs and claws are pure black. I don't migrate during the winter, since the cold weather doesn't bother me. I prefer to nest in a clump of trees, but I have been known to nest on top of electrical power transformers, too. When I locate a good-looking tree with plenty of privacy, it becomes my roost. I share this special place with other members of my family.

We eat an amazing variety of foods like cherries, acorns, walnuts, birds, eggs, spiders, earthworms, fish, and small mammals.

I have a sharp eye for fishing. I can pick a fish out of the water—even from a fast-moving river or stream. I let nothing go to waste. If I spot a dead fish floating in the river, dinner is served!

God thought of everything when he created me—**Carrion Crow.**

Tell a Friend

The Carrion Crow keeps his eye on everyone else's nest. People who spend all their time minding other people's business are sometimes called "snoops." In one of Paul's letters to the church at Thessalonica, he cautions church members to stay busy to avoid turning into snoops. His advice is good for us today, too.

Read About It

"Do everything you can to live a quiet life. Mind your own business. Work with your hands, just as we told you to. Then unbelievers will have respect for your everyday life."—1 Thessalonians 4:11, 12

The Bible mentions birds' nests in the New Testament when it describes Jesus as having no place to rest. Read Matthew 8:20.

Pray About It

Lord, help me to learn the difference between snoopiness and being genuinely concerned about others. Show me ways I can help those who need help.

Acrobat of the Air

If not for me, you'd have to put up with more flies and mosquito bites. I'm a glutton for mosquitoes, flies, and gnats, and my appetite helps control the number of those pesky critters.

Catching my dinner is no small task, but God equipped me with excellent vision. My eyes are made up of thousands of individual lenses, called facets, and are so big, they meet at the top of my head. I look like a set of flying eyeballs! I am able to detect even the slightest movement, so there's no use trying to catch me. I can spot you sneaking up on me from 40 feet away.

God designed four amazing wings for me. Delicately veined and transparent, they're not only pretty; they turn me into an agile acrobat. I'm among the fastest winged insects alive. My wings work together to help me accurately stop, start, and shift directions suddenly. Each set of wings works independently, too. I can flap them together, or one set at a time. It's not unusual to see my back wings flapping down while my front wings are lifting up.

Certain members of my family have been clocked at 36 miles per hour. My wingspan is about five inches wide, but scientists found a fossil of one of my ancestors with a wingspan of almost 30 inches!

The smallest of my species is from Borneo, with a wingspan of less than an inch.

God thought of everything when he created me—**Dragonfly.**

Tell a Friend

The Dragonfly's wings work together, and so can friends! Think of a time when you cooperated with a friend to accomplish a special project. How did it feel to see the end result?

Read About It

"Don't be proud at all. Be completely gentle. Be patient. Put up with one another in love."—Ephesians 4:2

Pray About It

Give me a heart that is willing to cooperate with others, Lord.

It is rare for members of my species to survive a whole year.

My Sticky Zigzag Surprise

Stand back, I'm a spitter! I belong to a family of six-eyed spiders. If you live in Singapore, I might have my eyes on you!

No need to worry. I'm harmless to humans, although if you stumble upon me in the night, it might be a creepy meeting. I'm a hairless spider that packs some very heavy equipment. I have a venom gland in front and a sticky-silk shooter in back.

While other insects sleep, I roam through the night hunting for a victim. In spite of all those eyes, my vision is poor, so God provided long sensory hairs on my feet. I crawl with my front legs raised, feeling my way around in the dark. Scientists believe that I am able to detect a victim nearby, as well as judge how far away it is, thanks to those hairs. I then react quickly—no time to waste!

I can attack a moth before it even knows I'm around by squeezing the back of my body together and spitting out two poisonous silk threads. I spit them in a split-second burst, zigzagging the strands over my victim like a fancy net. The sticky silk not only glues my prey in place, it paralyzes it so I can move in for a fatal bite. Once my victim dies, I then peel away the silk strands. Let the picnic begin.

God thought of everything when he created me—**Spitting Spider.**

Tell a Friend

The Spitting Spider creeps around at night seeking out something to devour. That's how Satan tries to catch us off guard. He wraps sin up in a pretty disguise and tries to tell us it's OK just this once. But God invites us to run to him when we are tempted. In him, we can find safety and rest.

Read About It

"So obey God. Stand up to the devil. He will run away from you. Come near to God, and he will come near to you."—James 4:7, 8

After laying eggs, my mother carried them around in her fangs for two weeks. Joined together by several silky strands, her precious cargo rode in what looked like a lacy little purse. I hatched two weeks later.

Pray About It

It is good to know that you are just a prayer away, Lord! When I am tempted, help me to turn away and run straight to you for help.

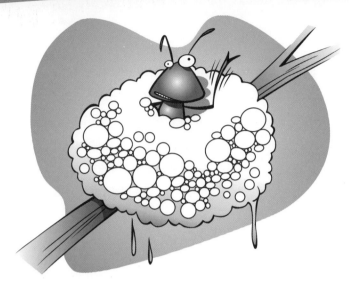

Protected by a Foamy Fort

A couple of months ago, my mother laid eggs on a leafy green plant. She chose a spot were her babies would grow safely. Inside my egg, I went through five stages designed by God.

God kept me warm and safe while I was a baby, called a nymph. He showed me how to produce bubbly foam mixed with air. I used the goo to build myself a fort for protection, by wrapping it around the stem of a plant. When my gob of spit reached the size of a large grape, I crawled inside. Inside my frothy fort, I was safe from predators on the prowl for a tasty snack.

My spittle fort kept me warm in cold weather and cool on hot summer afternoons. Moisture from the spittle also kept my body from drying out. Who but God could have thought of such a plan?

I didn't have a spine or wings in those early days, and as I grew,

I changed colors. I changed from yellow to green to brown. I'm now dark brownish black with bright orange stripes. My head is shaped like a frog's head, with dark eyes arranged at the sides. I have wings, but am also skilled at jumping, thanks to strong, springy hind legs.

God thought of everything when he created me—**Spittlebug.**

Tell a Friend

God created everything with an eye for detail. When's the last time you thanked him for taking such good care of you? He provides shelter, warmth, food, and so much more!

Read About It

"How good it is to sing praises to our God! How pleasant and right it is to praise him!"—Psalm 147:1

Pray About It

Lord, you provide exactly what I need for each day. Thank you!

It takes 45 to 52 days for me to turn into a winged adult.

Flightless Parrot of the Night

At eight pounds, I hold the title for the world's heaviest parrot. I am also one of the strangest and rarest birds in the world. You won't see me soaring through the air since I am a flightless parrot. I am also nocturnal, which means I am active during the night and sleep all through the day.

My scientific name is a mouthful: *Strigops habroptilus.* Aren't you glad your name is simple? My name means "owl-like," which is exactly what I am. My feathers are soft like an owl's, and I have a puffy circle of bristly feathers around my face.

When the first Europeans arrived in New Zealand around two hundred years ago, they brought along new animals like ferrets, weasels, and feral cats. These creatures hit the island running and soon developed an appetite for my family members. Since we are considered endangered animals, my little family now lives in a special habitat where we are kept safe and sound.

I have small, stumpy wings that are useless for flying. But when I am jumping down a steep bank, they sure come in handy for steering! People say I smell sweet and spicy, too.

God thought of everything when he created me—**Kakapo.**

Tell a Friend

The Kakapo is not a typical bird. It is a unique species—one of a kind. People are also unique. But we do have one very special thing in common: the need for a Savior. God knew our need and loved us enough to send Jesus for that very purpose! Read about it in the verse below.

Read About It

"God loved the world so much that he gave his one and only Son. Anyone who believes in him will not die but will have eternal life." —John 3:16

The Bible mentions feathers and wings in Psalm 91:4. Read what God says about his loving protection over us.

Pray About It

Lord, thank you for creating me as a unique individual. And thank you for sending Jesus to be my Savior.

Look, Ma! No Cavities!

I'm about one-third the size of a football field, with gill slits that wrap almost around my head. My most recognizable feature, though, is my huge mouth. I am a slow swimmer, creeping along at only three miles per hour.

I live by the buddy system, traveling in groups as small as 3 or 4, up to large schools of 100. But you can *relax!* We're harmless to humans. We travel the balmy waters off the coasts of both North and South America.

God thought of an awesome system for filtering water. I swim with my mouth wide open! Water flows into my mouth, along with plankton, fish eggs, and different varieties of baby fish. When I close my mouth, special spiky growths called gill rakers go to work. Like a sieve, they sort out only the food I want to eat.

I won't settle for breakfasting on cod or snacking on snapper—no, sir! Instead, I prefer plankton—tiny plants and animals that float along near the water's surface. Plankton supplies the energy I need to make my way through the water. If I find myself swimming in an area lacking in plankton, I will lose strength quickly and won't have enough energy to hold my mouth open while I swim.

God thought of everything when he created me—**Basking Shark.**

Tell a Friend

The Basking Shark isn't used to swimming all alone. Humans were not created to travel through life by themselves, either. We need each other, but even more: God knew that we would need a Savior, and sent Jesus. What does Jesus mean to you?

Read About It

"God's grace has saved you because of your faith in Christ. Your salvation doesn't come from anything you do. It is God's gift. It is not based on anything you have done. No one can brag about earning it."—Ephesians 2:8, 9

I am the next-to-largest fish in the sea, weighing in at over seven tons!

Pray About It

Dear God, thank you for providing what I need most—a Savior! Help me to travel side-by-side with Jesus all the days of my life.

Big Shot of the Forest

Scientists don't know whether to call me a plant, animal, or fungus. I live in rotting stumps and downed logs deep in the forest. I'm a member of a family known as slime molds. My family lives in every continent of the world, as part of God's design.

During a certain stage of growth, I send up tiny growths that resemble miniature mushrooms. In autumn, you will find me growing in neat rows along a downed tree or in the cracks of a stump. You might also find me growing under leaf litter or on large twigs scattered across the forest floor.

During my fruiting stage, I am filled with a creamy, slimy substance that resembles a thick milkshake. Hungry insect larvae love to scoop out my innards and feast on my scrumptious slime mold.

I change in size, shape, and color as I grow. My "costumes" range in color from gold to white to orange to brown. Photographers and painters have captured me on film and canvas. I'm sort of a forest celebrity, since I've been the star of many books and educational videos.

If I can escape those hungry insect larvae, I will live long enough to feed on decaying materials in the forest. What do you suppose would happen to all those rotting logs and stumps if it wasn't for tiny workers like me?

God thought of everything when he created me—**Ice-Cream-Cone Myxo.**

Tell a Friend

Each stage of a slime mold's growth brings about change. As we grow, we will also change in size and appearance. But the most important growth happens in our spirit, where only God can see. Are you learning to depend more on him each day?

Read About It

"Grow in the grace of our Lord and Savior Jesus Christ. Get to know him better."—2 Peter 3:18

Scientists are studying one of my slimy cousins to see how its cells grow, in hopes of understanding how diseases like cancer spread.

Pray About It

Give me a hunger for your Word, Lord, so I can get to know you better.

Index

African Grey Parrot 10, 11
African Jacana 62, 63
Alcon Blue Butterfly . . . 52, 53
Ambush Bug 74, 75
Anaconda 36, 37
Anglerfish 224, 225
Armadillo 16, 17
Asian Lady Beetle . . . 164, 165
Australian Scrub
 Turkey 176, 177

Babirusa 202, 203
Banana Slug 66, 67
Baobab Tree 20, 21
Basking Shark 240, 241
Black Mamba 126, 127
Blue Cheeked
 Bee-Eater 192, 193
Bombardier Beetle . . 218, 219
Bulldog Fishing Bat . . . 12, 13

Calvaria Tree 170, 171
Camel Spider 146, 147
Cane Toad 208, 209

Capybara 76, 77
Carrion Crow 230, 231
Cecropia Tree 130, 131
Chicken Turtle 70, 71
Chuckwalla 82, 83
Click Beetle 4, 5
Cobra Lily 8, 9
Cocklebur 228, 229
Copepod 172, 173
Crocodile 180, 181
Cuckoo Wasp 100, 101

Dall Sheep 116, 117
Dead-Leaf Mantid . . . 184, 185
Desert Locust 46, 47
Dragonfly 232, 233
Dung Beetle 60, 61

Eagle Owl 186, 187

Fishing Cat 124, 125
Fishing Spider 98, 99
Flamingo 196, 197
Flying Dragon Lizard 194, 195

Flying Tree Snake 86, 87

Giant African Stick
   Insect 106, 107
Giant Anteater 42, 43
Giant Antpitta 120, 121
Giant Australian
   Cuttlefish 214, 215
Giant Chinese
   Salamander 6, 7
Giant Grasshopper 26, 27
Giant Quaking Aspen 160, 161
Giant Red Mysid 174, 175
Giant Vinegaroon 78, 79
Goliath Bird-Eating
   Spider 72, 73
Goliath Frog 44, 45
Golomyanka 58, 59
Great Owl Butterfly   128, 129

Himalayan Griffon 18, 19
Hoatzin 28, 29
Honey Ant 108, 109
Housefly 24, 25

Ice-Cream-Cone
   Myxo 242, 243

Isopod 30, 31

Java Fiddle Beetle . . 122, 123
Jerboa 158, 159

Kakapo 238, 239
Kangaroo Rat 32, 33
Kea 198, 199
Kiwi Bird 148, 149

Lanternfly 212, 213
Laughing Kookaburra   94, 95
Leech 38, 39
Lion's Mane Jellyfish . . 90, 91

Madagascar Hissing
   Cockroach 182, 183
Mountain Zebra 80, 81
Mudskipper 156, 157

Naked Mole Rat 206, 207
Nile Crocodile 22, 23

Octopus 48, 49
Ornate Day Gecko . . . 226, 227
Oyster Toadfish 84, 85

Patas Monkey 178, 179
Peregrine Falcon...... 68, 69
Pitcher Plant 154, 155
Platypus 152, 153
Pompeii Worm...... 138, 139
Portuguese
  Man-of-War......... 34, 35
Ptarmigan 114, 115

Rafflesia Arnoldi...... 64, 65
Rhinoceros Beetle... 136, 137
Rizobium 220, 221
Rock Hyrax......... 144, 145

Satin Bowerbird 132, 133
Sea Bean 140, 141
Sea Cucumber...... 112, 113
Shrew 56, 57
Slime Worm........ 222, 223
Snowshoe Hare 102, 103
Sonoran Fringe-Toed
  Lizard 92, 93
South American
  Army Ant 162, 163
Spectacled Bear 96, 97
Spinifex Hopping
  Mouse 104, 105

Spitting Spider...... 234, 235
Spittlebug.......... 236, 237
Springtail 134, 135
St. Andrew's Cross
  Spider 200, 201
Stink Badger 40, 41
Strangler Fig 88, 89
Sundew............. 110, 111
Surinam Toad 50, 51

Tamarisk Tree 188, 189
Tarantula Hawk..... 166, 167
Texas Threadsnake.... 54, 55
Thorny Devil 168, 169
Tomato Frog........ 210, 211
Two-Toed Sloth 14, 15

Victoria Amazonica .. 190, 191

Wallace's Flying Frog 150, 151
Water Bear......... 118, 119
White-Throated
  Woodrat......... 142, 143
Wolffia 204, 205

Yucca Moth........ 216, 217

Scripture Index

Genesis 1:21 . . . . 84, 85

Genesis 1:24 . . . . 36, 37

Genesis 21:33 . . . . . . 188, 189

Exodus 8:1-15 . . . . . . 150, 151

Exodus 10:13-20 . . . . . . 46, 47

Leviticus 11:19 . . . . 12, 13

Joshua 1:9 . . . . 70, 71

1 Samuel 16:7 . . . . 28, 29

1 Samuel 16:7 . . . . 78, 79

1 Samuel 17:4-7 . . . . . . 44, 45

1 Samuel 17:33-37 . . . . 96, 97

1 Samuel 24:14 . . . . . 134, 135

2 Kings 17:39 . . . . 40, 41

Nehemiah 2:13 . . . . 60, 61

Job 7:5 . . . . 138, 139

Job 8:13-15 . . . . 200, 201

Job 15:23 . . . . 18, 19

Job 27:18 . . . . 216, 217

Job 28:1-7 . . . . 68, 69

Psalms 9:9 . . . . 68, 69

Psalms 18:30 . . . . 208, 209

Psalms 19:14 . . . . 90, 91

Psalms 19:14 . . . . 182, 183

Psalms 19:14 . . . . 192, 193

Psalms 22:6-8 . . . . . . 222, 223

Psalms 22:10 . . . . 156, 157

Psalms 23:3 . . . . 116, 117

Psalms 32:5 . . . . 198, 199

Psalms 32:8 . . . . 172, 173

Psalms 37:4 . . . . 76, 77

Psalms 37:39 . . . . 118, 119

Psalms 46:10 . . . . 10, 11

Psalms 56:3 . . . . 178, 179

Psalms 56:4 . . . . 4, 5
Psalms 64 . . . . 74, 75
Psalms 68:19 . . . . 158, 159
Psalms 78:46 . . . . 26, 27
Psalms 91:4 . . . . 238, 239
Psalms 104:18 . . . . 40, 41
Psalms 105:4 . . . . 98, 99
Psalms 108:3, 4 . . . . . 190, 191
Psalms 119:57 . . . . 6, 7
Psalms 119:66 . . . . . . 166, 167
Psalms 119:103 . . . . . . 56, 57
Psalms 119:105 . . . . . 224, 225
Psalms 119:114 . . . . . . 66, 67
Psalms 119:130 . . . . . 174, 175
Psalms 121:8 . . . . 140, 141
Psalms 139:14 . . . . 42, 43
Psalms 139:15 . . . . . . 180, 181
Psalms 139:15, 16 . . . . . 62, 63
Psalms 139:23, 24 . . . 162, 163
Psalms 143:10 . . . . 46, 47
Psalms 143:10 . . . . . . 170, 171
Psalms 145:13 . . . . . . 196, 197
Psalms 145:16 . . . . . . 142, 143
Psalms 147:1 . . . . 236, 237

Proverbs 3:5, 6 . . . . . 104, 105
Proverbs 4:18 . . . . . . 102, 103
Proverbs 6:6-8 . . . . . 162, 163
Proverbs 6:6 . . . . 108, 109
Proverbs 9:10 . . . . 48, 49
Proverbs 10:19 . . . . . . 18, 19
Proverbs 12:18 . . . . . . 94, 95
Proverbs 14:23 . . . . . 206, 207
Proverbs 15:1 . . . . . . 138, 139
Proverbs 15:4 . . . . . . 160, 161
Proverbs 16:3 . . . . 14, 15
Proverbs 17:17 . . . . . 100, 101
Proverbs 17:17 . . . . . 128, 129
Proverbs 17:17 . . . . . 220, 221
Proverbs 18:9 . . . . 14, 15
Proverbs 18:10 . . . . . . 92, 93
Proverbs 18:24 . . . . . . 26, 27
Proverbs 19:8 . . . . 50, 51
Proverbs 19:17 . . . . . . 20, 21
Proverbs 21:23 . . . . . . 30, 31
Proverbs 30:25 . . . . . 130, 131
Proverbs 30:28 . . . . . . 82, 83

Ecclesiastes 3:7 . . . . . 120, 121
Ecclesiastes 10:12 . . . . 72, 73

Isaiah 32:2 . . . . 106, 107
Isaiah 40:31 . . . . 194, 195
Isaiah 58:11 . . . . 164, 165
Isaiah 64:8 . . . . 44, 45

Jeremiah 17:7, 8 . . . . 188, 189
Jeremiah 29:11 . . . . 34, 35

Nahum 1:7 . . . . 222, 223

Matthew 3:1-6 . . . . . . 146, 147
Matthew 5:6 . . . . 12, 13
Matthew 5:43, 44 . . . . 226, 227
Matthew 6:25, 33 . . . . . . 38, 39
Matthew 8:20 . . . . 230, 231
Matthew 10:16 . . . . . . 126, 127
Matthew 14:14-20 . . . 224, 225

Luke 12:24, 25 . . . . . . 194, 195
Luke 15:3-7 . . . . 116, 117

John 3:16 . . . . 238, 239
John 4:24 . . . . 214, 215
John 7:38 . . . . 168, 169
John 12:46 . . . . 146, 147
John 13:34 . . . . 210, 211

Acts 2:44 . . . . 130, 131
Acts 14:17 . . . . 152, 153

Romans 10:12 . . . . . . 132, 133
Romans 12:6 . . . . 148, 149
Romans 12:10 . . . . . . 216, 217

1 Corinthians 3:9 . . . . 134, 135
1 Corinthians 10:13 . . 154, 155
1 Corinthians 10:13 . . 200, 201
1 Corinthians 15:58 . . 176, 177

2 Corinthians 5:17 . . . . . 22, 23
2 Corinthians 5:17 . . . 202, 203

Galatians 6:2 . . . . 52, 53

Ephesians 2:8, 9 . . . . 240, 241
Ephesians 4:2 . . . . . . 232, 233
Ephesians 4:31, 32 . . . . 82, 83
Ephesians 5:1, 2 . . . . . . 64, 65
Ephesians 5:1, 2 . . . . 212, 213
Ephesians 6:13 . . . . . 136, 137
Ephesians 6:14-17 . . 114, 115

Philippians 2:13 . . . . 24, 25
Philippians 2:13 . . . . 88, 89

Colossians 2:6, 7 . . . . 110, 111
Colossians 2:7 . . . . . . 160, 161
Colossians 3:12 . . . . . . 74, 75
Colossians 3:23 . . . . 60, 61
Colossians 3:23 . . . . . . 86, 87
Colossians 3:23 . . . . 124, 125

1 Thessalonians
  4:11, 12 . . . . 230, 231
1 Thessalonians 5:18 . . 16, 17

1 Timothy 4:12 . . . . 80, 81
1 Timothy 6:6-8 . . . . 32, 33

2 Timothy 3:16 . . . . . . 122, 123

Hebrews 2:18 . . . . 8, 9
Hebrews 4:12 . . . . 218, 219
Hebrews 10:23 . . . . . . 112, 113
Hebrews 13:8 . . . . 96, 97

James 3:9, 10 . . . . 54, 55
James 4:7, 8 . . . . 234, 235

1 Peter 4:10 . . . . 228, 229
1 Peter 5:7 . . . . 58, 59
1 Peter 5:7 . . . . 144, 145

2 Peter 1:3 . . . . 150, 151
2 Peter 3:18 . . . . 242, 243

1 John 3:18 . . . . 186, 187
1 John 3:18 . . . . 204, 205
1 John 3:20 . . . . 184, 185
1 John 4:12 . . . . 108, 109

Topical Index

Ability

Capybara 76, 77

Oyster Toadfish 84, 85

Fishing Cat 124, 125

Kiwi Bird 148, 149

Cocklebur 228, 229

Ambush

Ambush Bug 74, 75

Tomato Frog 210, 211

Anger

Himalayan Griffon. . . . 18, 19

Chuckwalla 82, 83

Pompeii Worm. 138, 139

Appearance, judging by

Hoatzin. 28, 29

Giant Vinegaroon. 78, 79

Armor

Rhinoceros Beetle   136, 137

Armadillo. 16, 17

Chuckwalla 82, 83

Giant Red Mysid . . . 174, 175

Bible (See also God's Word)

Bulldog Fishing Bat . . 12, 13

Surinam Toad 50, 51

Banana Slug 66, 67

Sonoran Fringe-Toed
  Lizard 92, 93

Sea Cucumber. 112, 113

Anglerfish 224, 225

Camouflage

Mountain Zebra. 80, 81

Care, God's

Click Beetle 4, 5

Kangaroo Rat 32, 33

African Jacana 62, 63

Crocodile 180, 181

Change, adapting to

Spectacled Bear 96, 97

Choices, making wise

Surinam Toad 50, 51

Communication

Laughing Kookaburra 94, 95

Rock Hyrax 144, 145

Contentment

Kangaroo Rat 32, 33

Cooperation

Rizobium 220, 221

Dragonfly 232, 233

Courage

Chinese Giant
   Salamander 6, 7

Direction, God's

Portuguese
   Man-of-War 34, 35

Discouragement

Slime Worm 222, 223

Disguise

Dead-Leaf Mantid . . 184, 185

Encouragement

Calvaria Tree 170, 171

Enemies

Stink Badger 40, 41

Equipping, by God

Giant Anteater 42, 43

Sea Bean 140, 141

Wallace's Flying
   Frog 150, 151

Example, setting

Mountain Zebra 80, 81

Eyes

Nile Crocodile 22, 23

Housefly 24, 25

Carrion Crow 230, 231

Dragonfly 232, 233

Father, caring

African Jacana 62, 63

Fear

Chicken Turtle 70, 71

Patas Monkey 178, 179

Feet, special design

Flamingo 196, 197

Food, spiritual

Bulldog Fishing Bat . . 12, 13

Fragrance

Rafflesia Arnoldi 64, 65

Friendship

Giant Grasshopper . . . 26, 27

Alcon Blue Butterfly . . 52, 53

Cuckoo Wasp 100, 101

Great Owl Butterfly 128, 129

Cecropia Tree 130, 131

Victoria Amazonica 190, 191

Tomato Frog 210, 211

Gifts (See Ability)
Giving
Baobab Tree 20, 21
God's Word
Chinese Giant
Salamander 6, 7
Bulldog Fishing Bat . . 12, 13
Spinifex Hopping
Mouse 104, 105
Java Fiddle Beetle. . 122, 123
Gossip
Texas Threadsnake . . . 54, 55
Growth
Ice-Cream-Cone
Myxo 242, 243
Guidance
Copepod. 172, 173

Habit
Snowshoe Hare. . . . 102, 103
Heaven
Kangaroo Rat 32, 33
Help, God's
Click Beetle 4, 5
Cobra Lily. 8, 9
Helping others
Springtail. 134, 135

Home
Kangaroo Rat 32, 33
Hunger, spiritual
Bulldog Fishing Bat . . 12, 13
Shrew. 56, 57

Identity
Babirusa 202, 203
Imitation
Laternfly 212, 213
Giant Australian
Cuttlefish 214, 215
Influence
Madagascar Hissing
Cockroach. 182, 183
Insect-trapping plant
Cobra Lily. 8, 9
Pitcher Plant 154, 155
Sundew 110, 111
Intelligence
Octopus 48, 49

Jealousy
Himalayan Griffon. . . . 18, 19

Kindness
Ambush Bug 74, 75

Light
Camel Spider 146, 147
Giant Red Mysid . . . 174, 175
Anglerfish 224, 225

Listening
African Grey Parrot . . . 10, 11
Portuguese
Man-of-War 34, 35

Material possessions
White-Throated
Woodrat 142, 143

Mouth, special design
Basking Shark 240, 241

Parasite
Isopod 30, 31
Cuckoo Wasp 100, 101

Partnership
Cecropia Tree 130, 131
Yucca Moth 216, 217
Rizobium 220, 221

Peer Pressure
Desert Locust 46, 47
Madagascar Hissing
Cockroach 182, 183

Perseverance
Tamarisk Tree 188, 189

Plan, God's
Housefly 24, 25
Portuguese
Man-of-War 34, 35
Dung Beetle 60, 61

Prayer
African Grey Parrot . . . 10, 11
Rock Hyrax 144, 145

Problems
Click Beetle 4, 5
Leech 38, 39
Peregrine Falcon 68, 69
Dall Sheep 116, 117
Tamarisk Tree 188, 189
Flying Dragon
Lizard 194, 195

Protection
Banana Slug 66, 67
Ptarmigan 114, 115
Cane Toad 208, 209
Spittle Bug 236, 237

Provision, God's
Armadillo 16, 17
Platypus 152, 153

Purpose

Housefly. 24, 25

Dung Beetle. 60, 61

Strangler Fig 88, 89

Asian Lady Beetle . . 164, 165

Responsibility

Australian Scrub

Turkey 176, 177

Root

Sundew 110, 111

Sea Cucumber. 112, 113

Giant Quaking

Aspen 160, 161

Salt

Tamarisk Tree 188, 189

Scripture

Java Fiddle Beetle. . 122, 123

Self-control

Goliath Bird-Eating

Spider 72, 73

Sharing

Baobab Tree 20, 21

Sin

Black Mamba 126, 127

Pitcher Plant. 154, 155

Spitting Spider 234, 235

Kea. 198, 199

Sloth (laziness)

Two-Toed Sloth 14, 15

Speech, guarding

Isopod 30, 31

Texas Threadsnake. . . 54, 55

Lion's Mane Jellyfish . 90, 91

Giant Antpitta 120, 121

Stubbornness

Tarantula Hawk. . . . 166, 167

Tail, special design

Ornate Day Gecko . . 226, 227

Temper (See Anger)

Temptation

Cobra Lily. 8, 9

Pitcher Plant 154, 155

St. Andrew's Cross

Spider 200, 201

Spitting Spider 234, 235

Thanks, giving

African Grey Parrot. . . 10, 11

Thirst

Giant African Stick

Insect 106, 107

Thorny Devil 168, 169

Tongue

Isopod 30, 31

Giant Anteater. 42, 43

Trouble

Water Bear 118, 119

Trust in God

Click Beetle. 4, 5

Uniqueness of individuals

Anaconda. 36, 37

Goliath Frog. 44, 45

Fishing Cat 124, 125

Kakapo. 238, 239

Vision

Carrion Crow. 230, 231

Dragonfly. 232, 233

Voice

Laughing Kookaburra 94, 95

Giant Antpitta 120, 121

Water

Thorny Devil 168, 169

Weakness

Fishing Spider. 98, 99

Weapons

Bombardier Beetle 218, 219

Weather

Giant Grasshopper . . . 26, 27

Wisdom

Octopus 48, 49

Surinam Toad 50, 51

Word, God's (See God's Word)

Words, choice of

Lion's Mane Jellyfish 90, 91

Laughing Kookaburra 94, 95

Words, encouraging

Isopod 30, 31

Words, hurtful

Goliath Bird-Eating

Spider 72, 73

Blue Cheeked Bee-

Eater 192, 193

Words, power of angry

Himalayan Griffon. . . . 18, 19

Work

Flying Tree Snake 86, 87

Naked Mole Rat. . . . 206, 207

Worry

Leech 38, 39